THE HIDDEN VOICES SERIES

A Working Life, Cruel Beyond Belief

Alfred Temba Qabula

HIDDEN VOICES

Second edition published by
Jacana Media (Pty) Ltd, in 2017

10 Orange Street
Sunnyside
Auckland Park 2092
South Africa
+2711 628 3200
www.jacana.co.za

First edition published by Numsa 1989
© Alfred Temba Qabula, 1989

All rights reserved.

ISBN 978-1-928232-31-5

Cover design by Shawn Paikin
Set in Stempel Garamond 10.5/14pt
Printed and bound by Creda Communications
Job no. 002919

See a complete list of Jacana titles at www.jacana.co.za

 HIDDEN VOICES

The financial assistance of the National Institute of Humanities and Social Sciences (NIHSS) towards this research is hereby acknowledged. Opinions expressed and conclusions arrived at are those of the author and editors and are not necessarily to be attributed to the NIHSS.

A Working Life,
Cruel Beyond Belief

Foreword

THE HIDDEN VOICES PROJECT EMERGED out of an interest in left intellectual contributions towards discussions on race, class, ethnicity and nationalism in South Africa. Specifically, the project seeks to examine and make available writings on left thought under apartheid. The aim is to look at hidden voices – voices outside of the university system, or academic voices suppressed by apartheid pressures. Before and during the apartheid years, many universities were closed to existing local ideas and debates, and critical intellectual debates, ideas, texts, poetry and songs often originated outside academia during the period of the struggle for liberation.

The Hidden Voices Series seeks to publish key texts, books, documents and other materials that were never published under apartheid, or seminal books that have gone out of print. We hope that these recovered, lost or forgotten voices will help reinvigorate the humanities and social sciences, and contribute to the decolonisation of knowledge production in South Africa and indeed throughout Africa.

It is a great privilege to launch our series with *A Working Life, Cruel Beyond Belief,* by Alfred Temba Qabula, with a new introduction by the original translator, B.E. Nzimande. Qabula was a central figure in the cultural movement among working people that emerged in and around Durban in the 1980s. It was an innovative attempt to draw on the oral poetry developed among the Nguni people over many centuries. Alfred Temba Qabula was a forklift driver in the Dunlop tyre factory in Durban at the time this book was developed. He used the art of telling stories to critique the exploitation of black workers and their oppression under apartheid. He was a grassroots intellectual, best understood as an organic intellectual, a notion developed by the Italian Marxist, Antonio Gramsci.

This book, and indeed the entire series, has been made possible by the generous support of the National Institute for the Humanities and Social Sciences (NIHSS). The Institute was established in December 2013 to advance and coordinate scholarship, research and ethical practice in the field of humanities and the social sciences (HSS). Its catalytic projects aim to encourage research in new areas of engaged HSS scholarship.

We would also like to thank Noluthando Mdingi, Alfred Qabula's daughter, and the original publishers, the National Union of Metalworkers of South Africa (Numsa), for permission to republish this book.

Karin Pampallis, Hidden Voices Project Manager, and
Edward Webster, Hidden Voices Project Director
November 2016

Introduction

IT IS A REAL HONOUR AND PLEASURE for me to be invited to pen this introductory preface to this new edition by this gallant cadre of the working class, Alfred Themba Qabula. I must note here that I accepted the offer to write this piece not just in my official capacity as a Minister in the African National Congress (ANC) government or as a leader of the South African Communist Party (SACP). I am grateful to write this introduction because I spent a good part of the mid 1980s and early 1990s with Alfred Qabula as part of the Culture and Working Life Project (of which I say more below), and also as an activist in ANC and later SACP underground structures. I also had the pleasure of translating into English some of Qabula's poems and plays as well as the *Cruel Beyond Belief* manuscript, which was originally published by the National Union of Metalworkers of South Africa (Numsa) in 1989. The process of doing this gave me extended opportunities for conversations with Qabula and insight into his life.

    I began my involvement with worker formations affiliated to the Federation of South African Trade Unions (FOSATU) around 1982, when I was doing my postgraduate studies in industrial psychology at what was then the University of Natal. I was introduced to Alfred Qabula and other workers at the Dunlop Tyre factory in Durban by Professor Ari Sitas around 1984. At that time Qabula, Mi Hlatshwayo and Gladman Ngubo were part of a cultural formation on the shop floor at Dunlop. Qabula and other workers at Dunlop were cultural expressionists, Zulu poets who used the art of telling stories to express and critique both workplace exploitation of African workers by capital and oppression by the apartheid regime. The approach eventually spread across factories in KwaZulu-Natal (KZN) and nationally. I was part of the interface between the cultural expressions of worker struggles and academia, which provided structural support to these formations.

I was part of the Culture and Working Life Project (CWLP) as a budding academic and activist with the Trade Union Research Project (TURP), housed in the Department of Sociology's Industrial, Organisation and Labour Studies Department. The CWLP was established officially in 1985 to provide training and give structural support to the growing expressions of workers and worker struggles through art, poetry, stage plays and drama. In KZN these activities were anchored in Sarmcol workers in Howick and Dunlop workers in Durban; this spread during the late 1980s to incorporate community struggles in Pinetown, KwaMashu and Pietermaritzburg.

Alfred Themba Qabula was a migrant worker, who worked at a Dunlop Tyre factory as a forklift operator, then became a trade union shop steward and later an organiser for the Culture and Working Life Project. In the 1980s Qabula became a playwright, poet, performer, organiser and a leading member of what became one of the most dynamic and innovative cultural movements in the country (Gwala, 1989; McGiffin, 2016; Nzimande, 1986, 1990; Sitas, 1989, 2002). But where did he come from? There are several stories about Qabula that feature prominently in his life as a worker leader and a cultural activist in the 1980s and 1990s.

Alfred Qabula was born in 1942 at Flagstaff in Pondoland. He describes the area where he grew up as a "harsh and beautiful land – a land of unending green hills and valleys, but also a land of poverty, of broken homesteads, of disease and malnutrition".[1] Qabula recalls a family history of proletarianisation, noting that his ancestors had ploughed the land for generations before capitalists came demanding labour for the mines and tax collectors came wanting cash. He recalls how his grandfather refused to be proletarianised, but when he could not resist any more sent his sons to work in the mines and sugar fields. Qabula recounts, "From then on migrancy invaded our home".

Qabula goes on to recount how proletarianisation affected his life growing up, which is also a typical story of migrant labour and changing household dynamics in many rural homesteads. His father, who was working in the mines, was a heavy drinker, a feature which, according to Qabula, was common among mine and industrial workers. He also notes that his father was a very harsh man "who coughed out on his family the bad treatment he received at work and on the streets of South Africa". He said of his parents, "My parents didn't just give us a good hiding, they would almost kill us if we did anything wrong".

---

1   Where no citation is given in the text, quotations by Qabula are taken from this book.

Frequently, the drinking and extreme violence resulted in his mother taking the children and running away to her own family.

In 1960 Qabula was introduced to the African National Congress. He witnessed violent suppression by the Nationalist regime on the people of Pondoland, and the subsequent hunting and killing of people associated with planned protests. These were struggles by local people against the Pretoria regime's imposition of the Transkei as an independent Bantustan. Qabula recounts a life as cruel as that of beasts. Many women reported that they were raped by soldiers. Soldiers also burned homes, plundered plantations and butchered livestock. Qabula himself found shelter and protection in the forest during those hard days. At that time, he also witnessed betrayal of communities by the local and regional chiefs, who sided with the Nationalist regime, and who sought protection from the apartheid government against the angry communities they had betrayed.

Qabula also experienced the harshness of migrant labour. He moved to Carletonville, where he worked as a plumber. Living in a hostel, he experienced the violence, squalor and dehumanising conditions under which black people lived and worked. He recounts how he survived two near-death experiences while in Carletonville, which made him look for work in Durban, following many other young men from his home town. Qabula found adult life to be even more complex and challenging than his childhood – the difficulties of finding work and of being an African worker during apartheid, harsh working and living conditions, and complex struggles of love, betrayal, witchcraft, marriage and raising children. He eventually moved to Durban, where he first worked as a plumber for a construction company, but in 1974 he left that job to work at the Dunlop Tyre factory.

It is interesting to see how all these aspects are woven into a tapestry of his life story, including his struggles and artistic expression through his poems, plays and *imbongi* songs. His poems and songs were not just a response to workplace exploitation and racial oppression under apartheid, but were a critique and reflection on the long history of colonial and capitalist resource extraction and environmental degradation (McGiffin, 2016). For instance, his 1984 poem, *You Moving Forest of Africa!*, is a poem about the rise of Fosatu (and the Metal and Allied Workers Union, MAWU) at Dunlop, a refuge for workers where they could be protected from exploitation and dehumanising shop-floor experiences (cited in McGiffin, 2016: 1). But trade unions were also becoming the nemesis of employers, who now looked to the state for support in crushing the rise of militant black trade unions. In his poem, Qabula presents trade union mobilisation as the forest, in which he and others found refuge in Pondoland when they were hunted and killed by soldiers during the Pondoland rebellion. But, as McGiffin (2016) shows, the allegory of the forest also addresses broader environmental issues, and shows how Qabula regards protection and preservation of human dignity, favourable work conditions and environmental conservation as part of a full circle of life.

Another poem, *Tears of a Creator*, which he composed with Mi Hlatshwayo and Nise Malange for the launch of Cosatu in 1985, is about the disappointment of betrayal. They speak of the betrayal of workers' struggles by the KwaZulu police, who were aligned with the Inkatha Freedom Party (IFP), and by local councillors and informants (askaris/impimpis) who sold out workers. The poem also addresses workers' struggles with management and the Special Branch of the South African Police. One gets a sense that Qabula in this poem is also recounting how the chiefs back in Pondoland betrayed communities when the Pretoria regime promulgated the 1959 Promotion of Bantu Self-Government Act. In this poem Qabula and his co-authors write, "But to our dismay, after we had appointed them, we placed them on the top of the mountain, and they turned against us. They brought impimpis into our midst to inflict sufferings upon us, some of us, those who were clever were shot down to the dust with bullets" (Qabula, Hlatshwayo and Malange, 1986: 12).

Before his death Qabula wrote *Of Land Bones and Money*, in which he critiques how South Africa's transition has created "winners and losers" among workers (cited in Sitas, 2003). He laments how some former worker leaders have abandoned workers, either when they were promoted to managerial positions on the shop floor, or when they took up political deployment in government. Interestingly enough, workers' awareness of potential betrayal by their own continued past Qabula's time; for instance, more than a decade after the achievement of democracy a Dunlop worker said:

Umuntusifikesimulwele, simxhase, umaelwanabaqashiukuthiaphakamiswe. Uma esebekiwephezulubeseyenafuthiasijikijelengamatshe. Uyababonanje, nalamaqabaneesawayisaepalamente, asesijikijelangamatshemanjesikhulumanje!

[We as workers fight for people to be promoted; all of a sudden once they have been promoted people throw stones at us, even comrades that we have deployed in parliament are now throwing stones at us.] (cited in Bhengu, 2014: 131).

Qabula was at the forefront of articulated struggles of workers, youth and communities against apartheid oppression. It is important to note that cultural expressions of poetry, stage plays, drama, music, photography and creative arts grew to become an important component of peoples' struggles in this period. Qabula, Mi Hlatshwayo and others in the CWLP were always part and parcel of struggle events, rallies and campaigns throughout the late 1980s and early 1990s. CWLP plays were used as a tool outside of South Africa to showcase atrocities of apartheid oppression and exploitation, as well as concerted struggles waged by workers, communities and youths for liberation. For example, a stage play by Dunlop workers was performed in several parts of Europe; some of these workers also joined Umoja and other cultural artistic groups that performed in many parts of the world.

Although Alfred Qabula worked as a forklift driver at Dunlop's factory, he composed while he drove his vehicle. He was an outstanding poet, with an amazing ability to conjure lyrics, words and expressions steeped in Zulu *imbongi* culture and styling, but at the same time narrating and traversing difficult and sensitive issues of workers' lives, shop-floor struggles and racial oppression under apartheid. His poetry and writing was significant in defining the terrain of struggles unfolding during the 1980s and 1990s. His involvement as a shop steward at Dunlop and his work with CWLP took place at a crucial time of contestation within the labour movement around the formation of the Congress of South African Trade Unions (Cosatu) and its subsequent drive to align with the Congress movement. During the mid-1980s, the contestations between "populist" and "workerist" unionism came to the fore. This was characterised on the one hand by a workerist faction that attempted to pursue a "purist" working-class organisation, concentrating only on shop-floor struggles. On the other hand, there was a stronger formation within the labour movement that saw workplace struggles, community struggles and the national democratic revolution (NDR) as closely related to each other. Qabula's writing clearly shows that workers on the shop floor were very aware of these contestations. Furthermore, his poetry and writing show that workers themselves conceived the workplace, the homestead, apartheid oppression and capitalism as an articulated whole. Workplace struggles were not just isolated class struggles; workers had a clear "historical materialist" conception of the working class – that is, working-class and poor blacks were oppressed by a cruel and unjust apartheid system of segregation and national oppression. In the songs, poems and political rhetoric, *abasebenzi* [workers] and *abantu* [people] were used interchangeably, just as *abelungu* [whites], *ongxiwa* [capitalists] and *abaqashi* [employers] were also used interchangeably. This is an important point, especially at the present time when there is yet another spurt of anti-Congress rhetoric from both ultra-left workerist formations and black chauvinists; they completely refute and ignore the persisting interplay between the class and national dimensions in contemporary South African struggles. It is important to note that whether we look at Alfred Qabula or Mzala Nxumalo or many others, they were very clear on the articulated nature of our struggle and of the NDR as espoused by the Congress Alliance.

Like many of our struggle heroes and heroines, Alfred Qabula was an organic intellectual of our struggle. Italian Marxist Antonio Gramsci, in his *Prison Notebooks* written in the late 1920s and 1930s, developed the notion of "organic intellectuals" who were embedded in and grew out of the working class. Qabula personified what Gramsci (1971) wrote regarding the importance of organic intellectuals and ideology for struggle. I personally believe that, had it not been for apartheid segregation and oppression, Qabula could very well have developed from shop-floor "grass root" to become a working-class scholar and intellectual, in the same category as well-respected American writer Harry Braverman. Perhaps he might have become a well-known and accomplished artist as well. In many ways, Qabula was a significant workers' intellectual, orator and poet. Through poetry and being involved in the Culture and Working Life Project, Qabula provided language and expression that reflected his analysis on a range of key issues facing workers on the shop floor and African working-class poor under apartheid oppression from the 1970s to the 1990s. Some seminal academic and intellectual writings by Ari Sitas, Debby Bonnin and others made use of Qabula's poetry in articulating concepts. For instance, Sitas (2004) uses Qabula's depiction of shop-floor struggles as *umlabalaba* (a traditional board game) to depict the complex nature of such struggles, characterised by victories and setbacks for workers and management alike. Qabula's poems feature in Sitas's (2004) seminal conceptual contribution to labour studies, *Voices That Reason: Theoretical Parables*. In this work Sitas brings together sociological and psychological streams of analysis in looking at everyday working life through the eyes of five different workers, from which he introduces what he calls "daydreams and reveries" as well as "cultural formations". The article explores in detail what he means by this, and examines the significance of oral poetry.

Reflecting back on the life, struggle and works of Alfred Qabula, two aspects have particular importance for our society today. The first is that Qabula and many others actively brought humanity back into spaces which the system had eroded. Racial segregation and oppression dehumanised our people, obliterated their sense of community, and undermined values and value systems that had been developed over generations. Furthermore, workplace regimes in South Africa dehumanised workers, turning them into mere tools of production and profit maximisation. Through cultural expressions, performance art, music and drama, a sense of humanity, a sense that workers, youths and communities were not just commoditised objects of political and economic exploitation began to permeate, especially during the mid 1980s and 1990s. Not only that, these artistic and cultural expressions also became the breeding ground for real expression of the values of a democratic, inclusive and non-racial society.

The second lesson is that stories about Qabula and many others of his generation highlight the richness of our indigenous cultures, languages and forms of expression. This is not only true for the arts and the kinds of artistic forms that give meaning to our people, but it also enables our artists to carve a unique niche in art forms internationally. Qabula's oratory, allegories and idioms used traditional *imbongi* styles of expression that resonated with the imaginations of migrant workers and communities across the country. Who can forget the international acclaim of Ladysmith Black Mambazo, who took a well-known migrant workers' musical expression of *ukukhala* (lamentation) – that is, *isicathamiya* (migrant workers' folk acapella music) – onto an international stage? Today they are celebrated as having won many international music awards, including three Grammy awards.

Based on these observations, I believe we need to have interventions and institutional mechanisms that will enable our society to consistently produce art and artists that give expression to our stories and our lives, and that nurture community and youth engagement in various forms of the arts and crafts. Earlier I argued that Alfred Qabula was an organic intellectual. This depiction is used to describe a number of worker, community and struggle cadres who developed through struggle to give a voice to our liberation struggle. But how do we establish systems and inculcate a culture that nurtures organic intellectuals? The answer lies in taking projects of reading and writing seriously, not just in our schools but also in our communities. This is why I am personally very passionate about establishing community and public libraries, community colleges and expanding the scope for lifelong education and access, as programmes that will build a culture of reading, writing and critical thinking from a community level. Such activities have the potential to become the breeding ground that produces engaged citizens and communities like those of Alfred Qabula.

Let Qabula and his poetry remain a symbol of the resilience of South Africa's working class, and inspire up-and-coming artists!

B.E. Nzimande
General Secretary, South African Communist Party
Minister of Higher Education and Training,
Government of South Africa
August 2016

REFERENCES

Bhengu, S. (2014) *Wage Income, Migrant Labour and Livelihoods beyond the Rural-Urban Divide in Post-apartheid South Africa: A Case of Dunlop Durban Factory Workers*. Unpublished PhD thesis, University of KwaZulu-Natal, Durban.

Gramsci, A. (1971) *Selections from the Prison Notebooks*. New York: International.

Gwala, N. (Nzimande, B.E.) (1989) Political Violence and the Struggle for Control in Pietermaritzburg. *Journal of Southern African Studies*, 15(3): 506–524.[2]

McGiffin, E. (2016) Iimbongi of the Resistance: Praise Poets, Trade Unions and Extractive Capitalism in Apartheid South Africa. *Green Letters*, DOI: 10.1080/ 14688417. 2016. 1163273.

Nzimande, B. (1986) Managers and the New Middle Class. *Transformation*, 1: 39–62.

Nzimande, B. (1990) Class Oppression and the African Petty Bourgeoisie: The Case of the African Traders. In *Repression and Resistance: Insider Accounts of Apartheid*, edited by R. Cohen, Y. Muthien and A. Zegeye. London and New York: Hans Zell.

---

2 This 1989 piece was written during the tenure of an oppressive apartheid regime and state-sponsored violence. It was common practice for anti-apartheid writers, scholars and activists to use pseudonyms for protection from persecution by the regime.

Qabula, A.T., M.S.D. Hlatshwayo and N. Malange (1986) *Black Mamba Rising: South African Worker Poets in Struggle*. Durban: Worker Resistance and Culture Publications, University of Natal.

Sitas, A. (1989) Class, Nation and Ethnicity in Natal's Labour Movement. *Institute of Commonwealth Studies: The Societies of Southern Africa*, 15(38): 267–278.

Sitas, A. (2002) Autobiography of a Movement: Trade Unions in KwaZulu-Natal 1970–1990. In *Culture in a New South Africa*, edited by A. Zegeye and R. Kriger. Cape Town: Kwela.

Sitas, A. (2003) Alfred Temba Qabula, 1942–2002: A Tribute. *Current Writings*, 15(1): 169–173.

Sitas, A. (2004) *Voices That Reason: Theoretical Parables*. Pretoria: University of South Africa Press.

Works of Alfred Themba Qabula translated by Blade Nzimande

Qabula, A.T. and M.S. Hlatshwayo (1986) Tears of a Creator: poem composed for the launch of COSATU. *South African Labour Bulletin*, 11(3): 61–68.

Qabula, A.T. (1989) *A Working Life: Cruel Beyond Belief*. Durban: Numsa.

Qabula, A.T. (1992) FOSATU. In *Words that Circle Words: A Choice of South African Oral Poetry*, edited by J. Opland. Parklands: A.D. Donker.

Preface

ARI SITAS SUGGESTED THAT I WRITE this book for everybody. My original plan was to write something only for my children, so if I died in one of my many migrant journeys I would not remain a stranger to them. They would turn to my notebook and learn that I was so and so who believed in this and that.

I would like to thank him and Debby Bonnin for making it possible for me to write this, get this translated and typed up. Here Chris, Makhi, Blade, Thomas and Norman must also be thanked for their translations; Steve Kromberg for editing and transcribing; Mathabo Olio and Deanne for proofreading. Also thanks to the History Workshop which encouraged me further by commending a section of this book for a prize in their working lives programme. This made me feel that even as a lowly worker I had something to contribute to the broader community.

Finally, to all the others who rallied to help me in these hard times, I wish to say that had I had a thousand mouths I'd make them sing their praises.

– *Alfred Temba Qabula*

This book is dedicated to the working people of South Africa, especially the migrant workers.

LIST OF POEMS

At the Dumping Ground 1

Mother 17

The Small Gateway to Heaven 59

In the Tracks of our Train 84

The Wheel Is Turning 118

Africa's Black Buffalo 132

At the Dumping Ground

1.
Whenever
    he has placed his creatures
    on the day of his calling
    they shall respond

Even at the dumping ground
    where there is filth piled up high
    alongside humanity's rejects and rubbish
    they shall respond

No one can muffle such a response
    by insisting that
    he was not calling
No one can silence the caller
    even if he was to be gagged
    if his eyes were shut
    his ears were blocked and his mouth
    stitched
    even if he was gaoled
    in a tightly sealed boxhouse
    so he heard nothing, saw nothing
    knew of nothing
    still,
    on the day marked by the call

his voice would sound through the lungs of this world
and the world would respond

2.
Because
    such a time has come
    miracles happen
    at the dumping ground
Sturdy trees
    with large and brilliant-coloured fruit
    emitting scents and beautiful to taste
    have grown
    and are available for free
at the dumping ground

But the farmers have assembled, worried
    asking each other
    who indeed dared to plant trees
    who dared to cultivate them
    to bear their fruit for free
        at the dumping ground?
    who dared destroy their monopoly of planting
    their right and their privilege to sell
    good fruit?

This new owner was a foreigner
    and an imposter:
    "let us destroy these orchards rooted in filth
        let us tear the trees down
        let us chop them to pieces and set them alight …
        let us destroy this abomination
        in our midst," they said

And so they did
    at the dumping ground

3.
And out poor black brother
    who sleeps in a scrapyard's Toyota
    nearby the dumping ground
asks in alarm

"Am I dreaming?
What do these eyes of mine see?
The world is beginning to blur in front of my nose
I can see
    the East and the West
    the North and the South
blurring together
in front of my eyes
I can see
    the mountains, the valleys and hills coming together
    the sun, the moon and the stars amassing
You cannot separate the sea from the rivers
    and waterfalls
Everything is blurring together and spinning
Am I mad or am I dreaming?
No, I am awake
    I am in my full senses!" …
"Have pity on me
    such a poor fellow
    born to be a victim of fear
    bred to be a victim of discrimination
I am scared …
Where am I to hide?

Nature is coming together
And I shiver whenever I stare
   at the dumping ground …"

"Oh!
   they have torn all the trees down
      at the dumping ground
   they have dug a deep hole
   they have chopped all the trees to tiny pieces
   they have poured paraffin and set them alight
   they have dumped and buried them in the deep hole
   they have stacked broken bottles
      old and rusted pieces of metal and iron rods
      and broken bricks on top
      to make sure they are never to grow
         ever again …"
"But my poor tired eyes
   what do they see?
Am I mad or am I caught
   in a dream
No.
   the trees are sprouting all over again
   and they are sprouting forth leaves
      what will the farmers say?
They are annoyed
   they are full of hatred
   they are furious
But the trees have more fruit
   more than ever before
Beautiful fruit sprouting out
   from this place of filth
At the dumping ground

They are greater than what the farmers yield
    and they are for free
    and the farmers' produce is going to rot
It has already started fermenting
    for people are gathering
        these free-fruit of filth
At the dumping ground."

We have come a long way
    with our efforts,
    with what we are doing
We have scraped through broken glass
    and sharp bottles
We have suppressed
    so we would ever dare raise our heads
We have broken through the rubble
    and we are making our very own world
At the dumping ground
    and we do not exploit
    and we do not cheat profits out of each other
we have slipped through their grip
leaving their cheeks blown up with anger
    and we are growing

We are responding
    and someone is calling
He is calling on us
    to work hard as daylight is coming
        it has been a very long sunset
        and a very long night
We are to sleep and listen to the voice in our dreams
    do not fear:

The one who is beginning to call
   is standing beside you
      with gifts and with infinite talents

Work on!

One

My name is Alfred Temba Qabula. When I started to write this book I had been working for 13 years as a forklift driver at the Dunlop factory in Durban. There, we made tyres of all kinds, of all sizes, for cars we never drive, for "kwela-kwelas" that chase us in the townships and belts for bulldozers that demolish our shacks.

I was a member of the Metal and Allied Workers' Union (MAWU), now the National Union of Metalworkers of South Africa (Numsa), an affiliate of the Congress of South African Trade Unions (Cosatu). Before that it was an affiliate of the Federation of South African Trade Unions (Fosatu). When the union was started in the factory I became a shop steward, a cultural activist and an oral poet (imbongi) in the Workers' Cultural Local in Durban. I now work full time as a cultural organiser, based in the Culture and Working Life Project at the University of Natal.

Together we are fighting, we are singing and we are uniting people to create a democratic South Africa without exploitation, oppression and fear.

My origins are simple: I was born on 12 December 1942, at Flagstaff, in an area called Bhalasi in Pondland. It is a harsh and beautiful land – a land of unending green hills and valleys but also a land of poverty, of broken homesteads, of disease and malnutrition.

My ancestors ploughed this land and trailed these hills with cow dung. They did so from way back, as far back as memory reaches in the clan of Miya; in the lines of Muja, of Sibweu, of Manqandanda, of Eluhluwini, of Sijekula, of Siyalankulandela, of Mancoba and of Henqwa. For two centuries their praise names and their cattle echoed around these valleys.

But then came capitalists demanding labour for the mines, and tax collectors wanting cash. My father's father refused to work on the mines and became a transport rider to raise cash to pay his taxes: with his ox wagon he footed the countryside from farm to farm, from the Transkei to Natal, from the Orange Free State and the Cape and back, carrying grain and other products. But he was destroyed by the arrival of the railways. He became a herbalist, and consistently refused to go out and work for a wage. He sent my father and his brothers out to work on the mines or in the sugar fields. From then on migrancy invaded our homes.

Two

I NEVER KNEW IT WOULD be so hard to be an adult. I began to be aware of things at the age of seventeen, in 1959, when there was general talk in the countryside about the trials and tribulations of the African National Congress.

In 1960 there was a big meeting about the troubles that befell us with people from different regions in Pondoland. It was to take place on Nquza Hill. So many people attended that a loudhailer had to be used; I could not estimate the number. The Nationalist regime's soldiers were also present on that day. Helicopters, armoured cars, army trucks, fighter planes of all kinds were there too.

When the meeting was about to start, the Boers called a big chief of the area. They asked him if he could see that his people were gathered for a meeting of the ANC. "What do you have to say?" they asked him. "What should we do to them?" He took a rifle and shot a man dead. He shot this man from the air while sitting with the Boers in a stationary helicopter. This act triggered off a riot. It triggered off the Pondoland rebellion.

Smoke blackened the sky. Fire broke out. A stampede.

Bombs ploughed the earth. You could hear people crying and screaming. Some of the crowd fled, some tried to thwart the attack using their sticks and stones. But this proved too little against the attackers.

The sorrow, the misery of that day is always remembered by those who were present and by those who were told by those who had been there. What followed thereafter was a life as cruel as that of beasts. Many women reported that they were raped by soldiers. The soldiers and informers burnt houses. They plundered stock. They butchered it in front of their owners. When they came across a person they asked him, "ipi lokhongo" – "where is congress?" People were being beaten up. Some people died from the violence, beaten to death. We did our best with knobkerries, spears and stones, but we were defeated.

People slept in the veld, in the forest, deserting their homes. I shall have occasion later to speak of the forest that gave me shelter and protection during those days of hardship.

The Boers divided the people in two: there were those who helped them burn the houses of Congress members. There were also those who had joined Congress and who burnt the houses of those who did not join. People brutally killed each other. Congress people gathered and attacked Botha Sigcawu's house. He ran away, hiding from place to place until he reached Lesotho.

The government sent protection for Sigcawu's place. They hired informers. There was a night and day patrol around the house. Many chiefs sought such protection. One of them was Chief S. Ntabankulu in Flagstaff near where we lived. It was the first time in my life I had seen such a bad situation. For three years, 1960, '61 and

'62 times were hard. Life became better in 1963 as bitter people returned to their fields.

But the issue of the Trust became the talk of the day in the Transkei. People had joined Congress because through it they wanted to unite, to have one voice to speak for them to the government who had bought over the chiefs. The chiefs had agreed to the Trust, a genocidal Trust which plagues the Transkei to this day. We were not prepared to move from our places, leaving the graves of our ancestors behind. The chiefs who did not agree to sell out were persecuted. Some were or are exiled. They attempted to shoot the chief of the Mpondos. They finally gave him the slowest killing poison so that he died banished. His cattle and other possessions were stolen.

We left our homes and found new homes in the forest. During the daytime we always stayed in the forest until dark. Then we divided ourselves into two groups to patrol around our homes and to check if everything was still in order. There were comrades in the police force who used to inform us when there was going to be an attack. I remember three police who lost their job because they passed information to us.

The people would divide themselves into two groups; one group to face the attackers and the other group to go and burn the attackers' houses. That idea came after a long period of not paying revenge to the attackers and after many members' homes were destroyed by amajendevu (informers), the army or the police.

The locals sat down and debated the issue. They agreed that all the locals must use this strategy. People were elected who would try to get information about what was going to happen each day, and when the informers and the system were going to attack us.

For a time, people were very active burning the amajendevu's houses and killing them. Then the amajendevu started to pull back and stay at their homes, trying to protect their belongings. Their things were taken as they had taken ours. When it became 50-50 they sent a delegation of six men to negotiate peace.

They were told that the people were not fighting with them but with the enemy who killed us, raped our women and destroyed our homes. The had pulled away from us and joined the enemy. They were the ones who made our lives so strange. Some of us had lost our homes through them. They were the people who informed the enemy about our strategy and they were the ones working with the white government to oppress our people.

Our demands to the government were: we should not be moved from where we were; they should not separate Transkei from South Africa as a puppet state; we did not want their 'betterment system'; South Africa is one and the government must not divide it into many weak states of puppets. If they wanted to free South Africa, they must free South Africa as a whole, black and white. And we said we had the right way to control South Africa. We told the informants that they must not be a stumbling block on our way to freedom.

After that delegation meeting there were fewer attacks and less violence, although there were still attacks by police and soldiers. I remember one occasion where one of the Zionist priests had a big rondavel which was waiting for the roof to be done. There was a helicopter which was used by the police and the army to trace the Congress people in the forests and over the mountains. This helicopter was a small little thing, its canopy like a bottle in which you can see the people while it is moving high. I think it takes three to four people at a time.

As we used to go to our homes to check if things were still in order, the Zionist priest went to his home, also to change his clothes and get clean clothes. While he was changing the police came and arrested him. He was surprised to find that the half-done house for the church was the garage for the little helicopter. They arrested him and took him to prison. He was questioned and after six weeks they released him and told him to stay at home, not in the forest. They said he was to pray for people to understand that the government was the way to civilise the Transkeians, and that he must preach this as well. He reported to us what had happened to him.

At that time things were impossible for us. We couldn't eat good food. Sometimes we ate fruit, some kind of roots or plain cooked mealies. Sometimes we ate stiff pap. We drank water to survive. We would say: "Thank you God, I have eaten decent food today." It was difficult to grind mealies on the grinding stone or to make a fire because the enemy would have seen where we hid ourselves and attacked us.

At school it was difficult for boys of my age. I was 18 years old when it started and most boys my age were members of the ANC Youth League. We were very active in the movement at the time. It was very difficult for us to go back to school, although the teachers were activists of the ANC, as were most of the chiefs. In 1962 we returned to school – but not every day. When we were informed that the police were coming, we hid in the forests. There was a time when we took our lessons in the forest to prepare for the examinations.

We were told that all the Youth League members were going to be trained to use guns, inside the country, by the Russians. Then they told us that we had to leave the country for training. In our area not a single person was trained.

I think that is why the Pretoria government decided to send the army into the Transkei – to stop the Russians from coming into the land and spoiling their slaves to rebel against them. There were some people who told us that Russian submarines had been seen in the South Coast sea, in places like Lambasi, Mkambathi, Mboyti and Port St Johns. I am not sure about this, although because of what I have said I think it did happen. If not, why did the Pretoria government send such a strong army? And why was the State of Emergency declared? That is why I believe that the Russians were around in the sea.

There were many things happening in the country which did not appear in the newspapers. The State of Emergency did not allow them to publish the reality. The formation of Umkhonto we Sizwe took place after the Pretoria government banned the people's movement, the ANC, and declared war against the people; after many shootings and killings; after much violence had taken place in the country.

I became an adult in these years of hardship, my soul awakening to a world cruel beyond belief.

Three

BEFORE I TELL YOU ABOUT my working years, I must take you back to my childhood. This was not without its hardships.

I was taught to respect my elders, the hard way. Of course, I tried my best to keep out of mischief. You see, my parents didn't just give us a good hiding, they would almost kill us if we did anything wrong.

My father's name was Solomon and my mother's name was Nonkululeko. My father was a miner at Egoli (Johannesburg). He worked underground, as a machine handler. He was a very strict man, had a short temper and loved his drink. Like many other men, he would cough out to his family the same bad treatment he received at work and on the streets of South Africa.

He died drinking: somebody poisoned his drink and he died belching out blood one Christmas – I think in 1949. The story goes like this. He went to visit his friends for a drink as usual. It was a rather cold day, the weather was bad and I was home that day. I was helping my mother to brew beer – and she was teaching me how to brew it.

While my mother was looking through the window, she saw two men carrying my father by his arms, taking him to my grandfather's house. She took a bucketful of water, washed herself, and decided to go there and find out what was happening. On her way to my grandparents' place she met the local doctor driving his car. The doctor gave her a lift to the old people's place. But they arrived there too late. He was still warm but they had missed him – he had gone resting. He had vomited a lot of blood.

Later the doctor checked his body, opened him up and found that he had been poisoned. His intestines were all messed up; they had been severed. I remember his funeral: a cow was slaughtered; for his safe journey, the old men said. I also remember that during the burial I did not cry. However, when I noticed my mother wearing black, I was overwhelmed, or scared, and started sobbing uncontrollably.

The case of my father's death was contested at the Flagstaff magistrate's office. Two men faced charges of fatally poisoning my father. One of them shared our surname and the other one came from the Mtambo clan. After a two-year-long battle they were acquitted. Not guilty and discharged. I am still in the dark – to this day I do not know what the trial was about. The world of adults conspired to keep it a secret.

From then on we could not afford an independent homestead so we moved to my grandparents' place. But my mother decided it was not nice there so we went back home and started from where we had left. We sold one cow in order to get enough money to live. We were left with two. My mother, before long, and without warning, developed a very urgent approach to our lives.

"I want to teach you domestic work so that you can cook and take care of your siblings when I'm gone. It will be difficult for you if I die," she said to me. One day I asked her why she never asked my younger brother to help with the household duties. She said she always asked me because when she was pregnant with me she thought she was carrying a girl.

Every Saturday I used to wake up early in the morning, make the fire, collect some firewood, fetch 20 litres of water five times, grind samp, make mahewu (sour porridge), polish the five huts with cow dung, chop wood and then sweep our yard.

After this my mother would say, "Thank you, my Miya (my surname). You can go now, you can go play stick fighting with your peers; you have finished what I wanted you to do for me; you are free to go now." And without further warning she died. Though she had been very sick she wilted without showing the slightest sign to us.

My mother had tried by all means to make sure we never lived like poor fatherless kids.

Mother

Even though I cannot see you through
    these natural eyes
I can see you through my
    imagination
The Lord only gave you a short span of years
And then you left for the land of the high
    winds
Long before I came to appreciate
    your presence

You left me
   with endless years of solitude,
But still I hear that soft
   echoing voice
guiding my way forward

Yes, Mother, all this leaves
   me with a question –
What is a home without a mother?

When I am away, out on the road
   Hungry, thirsty and full of tears
I think about you Mother
   and I regain my strength
M hunger, thirst and exhaustion disappear
The road's sorrows and worries
   disappear as I reach out
For you
My mother

Your word is the light in this
   world of darkness.
In times of war, your counselling
   becomes
      the weapon
      I conquer with.
Even in my solitude I do not
   feel lonely
      because of your instruction and lessons.
Though you left me rather early
   before I came to appreciate your presence.
   I say I don't regret.

The time had come for you to
    pass on to the land of the high winds
There too, your good work was needed,
    my Mother
Now Mother
    you must feel free
for your nation is feeling that way too.

Four

I cannot remember my father well. I only have a faded picture of him in my mind. He stayed on the mines for long periods. We never saw him much. All the cattle, sheep and goats he had, he bought with the money he earned down in the mines in Johannesburg, where the walls were singing.

His life remained vague to me and filled with rumour – that he belonged to gangs in Johannesburg, that he was a cycling champion out there, that he was a good man and a rebel. All I remember is his shambok and his horse's gallop. Though I can't remember what I had done wrong I can still recall all those days when he was chasing me on horseback – to kill me, I thought.

People in the neighbourhood used to stare at us in sheer amazement. On many occasions they must have thought it was all over with me. But I was clever, for I used to make sure I ran towards places where it was impossible for a horse to go. It was then too much of a bother for my father to climb off his horse to chase me. Of course, he also knew that when it came to running his son was equipped with a jet engine. Resigned to such facts, he used to climb off his horse then, pick up a couple of stones and throw them at the horizon.

I remember one time when he actually dived at me from his moving horse and got me. That day he bruised me badly with his shambok. Fortunately, I managed to slip from his grip and run for my dear life. I hid somewhere inside a Mission garden. He went around looking for me, shouting that it was all over, he was not going to beat me up any more, so I must come out from wherever I was hiding. I never stirred. I only came out after I was sure he had gone. I saw him moving homeward and I came out of my hiding place and used only secret footpaths on my way back home. Then I waited, like always, until the call of the brandy compelled him to go on his drinking sprees; then I would quietly go home.

My mother would always stand outside waiting for me, staring in the direction I had run. I was also scared of her as she was a bit like my father as far as beatings were concerned. She saw me coming that night and called my name.

I didn't trust her much. I went to her warily after studying her face closely. To my surprise her eyes were full of tears. She looked over my wounds: I was blue with shambok marks. She boiled some water to clean me and soothe the pain. Before long, my father returned to check if I was back already. My mother was furious, she was mad. She started shouting at him, asking him why he always made his children into the area's laughing stock and why did he treat us the way he did.

That is how they used to be: he used to explode on us and hold us responsible for his harsh life, of which we knew nothing. He and our mother would never stop quarrelling, but he never beat her. Anyway, that night I was in pain. It got really bad. I cried during the night. My father woke up, made up the fire and boiled some water to soothe my sores.

From then on, my health deteriorated. For some mysterious reason, after the beating I became a very sickly child. I couldn't keep anything in my stomach. My stomach was running for a very long time.

I was consumed by pain all over my body and spent most of my time doubled up and vomiting out whatever I was given to eat or drink. My elders felt scared so they took me to a traditional medicine man. He revealed to them the cause of my illness. They understood his words but I was never told anything. All I can still remember is that my mother brewed a lot of traditional beer for a ceremony. My father slaughtered a goat and apologised to the ancestors, asking them to restore my health. I was not given any herbs or medication. People gathered for the ceremony and enjoyed the meat and drank the bear; the ancestors accepted the apologies and I had my health restored.

One day, my brother and I were at home with our mother, sitting around and talking. My father was back from the mines and had gone out drinking. When he came back, he burst through the entrance of the hut drunk, waving his shambok. After an exchange of words, he started whipping us with the shambok.

He scattered us out of the hut and all over the fields. In fact, we made it out because our mother dived at him and wrested away the shambok for a short time. My father didn't sleep at home that night.

My mother woke us up in the morning. She washed and dressed us, packed our clothes and gave each one of us a piece of luggage to carry. I didn't know where we were going. She was silent, speechless, she told us nothing. She ordered us to walk. We walked and walked for a very long distance. I got very tired; my mother carried me on her back. We came to a railway coach stop. A bus drove by, so full of migrant people coming home that there was no space left for us. We walked on until it got dark.

We came to a house with many dogs. My mother asked for a place to sleep. The people of the house were very hospitable. They gave us shelter and before we slept even gave us a dishful of boiled dry mealies. We didn't eat much of the dish; the corn was dry and wasn't very palatable to say the least. The woman of the house asked my mother why we ate so little, to which she replied that her children were not used to eating dry food.

I slept early because I was tired but I woke up in torment. I couldn't get much peace in sleep; the dogs kept on barking. Some people went past the house. The man of the house went out and talked to them. I ended up sitting. Both the night and my mind were restless.

Early in the morning my mother thanked the people of the house for their kindness and off we went. This time we got the bus to Port St Johns. When we got there it was late again and we missed the only bus going our way. We ended up sleeping at some place called Khayeni, where we could also get something to eat. In the morning we woke up and had some porridge for breakfast. I could hold down nothing of this breakfast. My mother gave me some water to drink and to wash my face with. We took a bus and dropped off at the Mngazi River.

We walked for about a mile. We reached a house. There was an old woman standing outside looking at us. She was our grandmother. Everything there seemed so warm and so different from the house we had slept in the first night. She killed a cock and we ate a meaty meal for a change. I enjoyed a very peaceful sleep. By the next day all the extended family from my mother's side started arriving to welcome us. They were all so happy to see us. We soon became friends with the children next door and played with them. They took us to the beach and taught us how to swim. We went fishing and bird hunting. The distance from my granny's place to the beach was only a mile and a half.

We spent a very happy time at my grandmother's house. A goat was slaughtered for us. We forgot about the hunger way back at home in Flagstaff, at Bhalasi area. If I'm not mistaken, we stayed there for three weeks.

I remember, one day we had gone to the beach as usual; the sun was very hot and I got tired, so I returned home and fell asleep. It could only have been late morning. When I woke up I couldn't believe my eyes. My father was right there in front of me. He asked me what I was doing there and he asked why I left the sheep and goats alone way back home. I got very scared and forced my way out of the house and ran to where my granny was.

I told her that my father had arrived with his long shambok on horseback. I told her I was very scared because he might beat us again. My granny told me to take it easy since my father had not come to hit us, but he was visiting. My uncles came in to see him. Every member of the family came. They sat there and talked, my mother reporting everything he had done to us. He was given a warning by my uncles and promised not to misbehave again. We stayed for three more weeks, which made a total of six weeks. On the last week a goat was slaughtered and we were given some meat for the road. We wore new clothes that granny had bought for us. Real gentlemen we were! I was even wearing a bow tie.

On the way back I nearly drowned in a river. My brother and I were on horseback and our parents on foot. When we crossed a river the horse jumped over and we fell into the water. I was helpless since I couldn't swim well; I was still very young. My father took some time to come to my rescue. In the end he managed to pull me out of the water, took off my clothes and gave me a new suit to wear. I had a lot of clothes those days. We slept at my aunt's house (my father's sister). The next day we were home at Flagstaff at Siphaqeni. The next door neighbour had taken care of all our livestock, Mr Phungula by name. I went straight to my friend to tell him about my stay at Port St Johns and the new friends I had met there.

We had a relatively peaceful stay at home during the first few days. However, as time went on my father started being rude, scolding us for almost nothing. One day I really got mad and decided to tell him off. I said to him, "Look here, dad, you are starting with your flings now; you scold us for nothing, you want to beat us up for nothing. We are going to leave you alone with your house and your livestock and go to granny's house again. We'll never come back here again. Don't forget granny and my uncles are very strong. They will beat you up to nobody's business."

He just looked at me and laughed. From then on he never gave us trouble.

Five

YOU MUST ALSO UNDERSTAND that when I say I didn't like to get into mischief, I don't mean I was a "goody goody" or that we as children were little saints. We were up to mischief quite often.

I can still vividly remember one day I was sitting outside in the yard with my friend, and we got very hungry and decided to steal some eggs. My mother was cooking samp outside. She used dried cow dung as coal. We looked around the cattle enclosure to find some fresh (wet) cow dung and wrapped it around the eggs and stuck them into the fire. Mt egg was ready earlier because I had put it at the centre of the fire. We divided it between the two of us and ate it. I then took my friend's one and put it at the centre. But just before it was done my mother showed up and caught us red handed. "Oh," she said, "Is this the reason why you are so mindful of the fire?" We didn't wait for the rest, we just ran away. She started shouting at us and another man nearby tried to get hold of us but to no avail.

We crossed the Welakabili River, ran through the maize fields. We ran until we reached a field of sweet potatoes. We forgot that we were being chased and that the shouts were coming from a man chasing us to take us to my mother. Rather, we looked around for some digging objects, got a stick and helped ourselves after a bit of digging to some sweet potatoes. The man who was chasing us stood there laughing uncontrollably and holding his sides. He could not believe his eyes, that the kids he was chasing for stealing eggs were now stealing again. This was ridiculous, he said and left us there.

We roamed about until late afternoon. We got hungry and went to my friend's house. We were given food and we ate there. He had to walk me home. Now there was a problem; I had done something wrong so I knew the stick was awaiting me. My mother refused to give us food, saying that she hoped we were still full from the meal of eggs and potatoes we stole. We promised never to steal again so she forgave us, gave us supper and warned us that should we ever do this again she was going to call the police to arrest us. We did not tell her that we had already got food at my friend's place.

The following day, as we were driving the cows from the kraal to the meadows we saw a policeman! Horror-struck, we ran for our lives thinking they had come for us. Seeing us running like that made him follow: he dropped from his van and started chasing us. We hid in the thicket, panting. He spent 15 minutes looking for us until he eventually gave up the search and went. Life was back to normal. I didn't imagine then that such chases would be part of my normal adult life later.

To be truthful about our childhood, mischief and nonsense followed us most of the time. I remember how one day in winter we were playing at building sledge hammers from dry maize stocks. Something fell on one of my friend's head. He fainted. We suspected that someone threw a stone at him. We ran away and left him there. His mother and granny fetched him and took him to an inyanga. He stayed there for quite some time, until he got well. But I still feel guilty whenever I remember our leaving him there to die.

One of the most thrilling places of childhood was the forest, or better the forests, around our area. They were places of games and danger, places that were reputed to have supernatural and real forces that terrified you. They were the homes of pythons and adders and of wild beasts. They were the places inhabited by all the dreadful creatures your grandmothers spoke of in their stories. But to a child they were also places of learning: to survive by watching birds, eating their berries, or following the honey bird to lead you to honey, or hunting the birds to eat. When the Pondoland 'rebels' were being hunted and our lives were in danger, we sought refuge in the forest. We could survive in it because it was marked by the paths and the hunts of our childhood.

We used to do a lot of bird hunting when we were young. We collected a lot of stones and, armed with our slings, we would start at a forest called Zintwala and then go to a small thicket called Ezinqayini. In this thicket there was an enormous tree. At the trunk of this tree there was an enormous groove. On one of those expeditions I peeped into this groove and inside I saw a calabash covered by an enamel plate. I got very suspicious and half frightened: could this be a human being's meal or was it a trap set up by ogres? But still I was curious to see what was inside the calabash, despite my fears, despite also the old women's tales. I took heart and drew closer to the pot.

I first removed the wooden spoon on the plate, then the plate. It was full of amasi (sourmilk). I stirred the content with the wooden spoon and found that the sourmilk had ground cornmeal in it. I felt the pangs of hunger and then I wondered: "What must I do?" I asked myself: "Should I eat it?" But then again: "Who put the calabash there? Could it be that it was left there by some spirits? Could that curse befall us?"

I ended up eating the food. I felt courageous for I decided that if I was to die, then I was to die and so be it. It would be a solitary death and would affect no one else. I promised that I would not lift a finger from my coffin; it would be just the death of a single child. I took a deep breath and ate hastily, looking left and right, to and fro just in case the owner of the calabash arrived. But there was too much food there, so as I had my fill, I started calling my friends: I whistled, they whistled back. They came and asked where I got the calabash from. However, before I could answer them and explain to them the dangers involved they leapt at the calabash and with their hands working at great speed they finished all the food.

As they wiped their faces and were ready to go a huge boulder crashed in front of us. We started running out of the forest, with a volley of rocks and stones following on our heels. Fortunately none of us got hit. We couldn't, however, make out our assailant. We went back where the cattle were grazing, stunned by the strange episode. I requested that we stop talking about this calabash story lest it end up in the ears of the elders. I had this picture of all the elders in our village placing their sticks on our backsides. Frightened, we gathered the cattle and drove them back home. It was already getting dark.

Three days later my parents asked me to tell them all about the amasi-in-the-calabash story. There followed sharp reprimands about touching strange food.

But you never learn: you move through your childhood years feeling constantly hungry, so you move like a locust. Soon after the incident, while looking after the sheep and the goats, we went to a waterhole to drink some water. When we got there we found the carcass of a sheep. We promptly decided to eat it. I immediately set to work to make a makeshift knife out of a piece of tin. We skinned it after great effort and started to cut and work on its intestines. Most of the inside parts were braaied immediately. We then decided to equip ourselves better for the next day's feast: we were to bring a big tin to cook in, salt, a box of matches, a stack of firewood and knives. We then took the rest of the carcass and hid it behind a bush somewhere.

By then my little brother, who was tagging along for the day, became tired and homesick and demanded to return home. We pulled him by the ears, warning him never to say anything about the meat to my mother.

The problem started when my mother wanted to give him food. He declined to eat, saying that he was full from the braai from the carcass of a sheep. I returned home that evening, locked the sheep and goats in their respective kraals, and carefree I entered the door. I could instantly detect that the atmosphere was tense. I surmised that the cat was out of the bag. I was ready for anything.

I was given supper, and I ate my fill. My mother began to ask me why I did not tell her about the braai in the veld. She told me never ever to eat meat from a dead animal if we don't know what killed it. It might as well be that it was poisoned, she said, in which case I would be poisoned as well. I was lucky once more to escape the stick.

Despite hardships, my childhood and youth were full of adventures and challenges at school, in the veld, everywhere, where we used to get up to fights for no reason at all. What the problem or the cause of any fight was, nobody could tell. There was a time when we fought boys from Gabheni. It was a long feud, an almost traditional war of the boys. Sometimes we would quarrel over the use of the river. Sometimes we would demand that they did not swim before us since they would spoil the water for us. They never used to take that lying down and everything would end in a fight.

But such fights could become quite serious: one day while we were swimming these boys crawled behind a bush, stalking us as it were. We only saw them when they were very close to us but we managed to grab our sticks, and the fight lasted for hours, literally until the cows had come home. We defeated them and scattered them in all directions. Bu the next day they came back with more boys from Mthwaku. That day some of us got injured. Even then we managed to chase them and got hold of three of them and did everything we wanted with them, beating them up with sticks. We did this until the elders came and took them. For quite some time, they avoided our river and used others elsewhere. The feud among the boys continued until the early 1960s. As a boy you were born into one of those groups.

It's over now because many people were resettled during the establishment of the so-called betterment schemes and trusts. A lot of people moved from Bhalasi to Sigubudwini River. Some moved to Gabajani, some to Mthwaku. Now people have fenced paddocks where they all take their livestock. It's quite different from the olden days. It was fun to be a herdboy; we loved the fights and the adventures in the wild. That is where we got to know the heroes of childhood. We used to know that so and so is an expert at stick fighting, so and so is a coward, and so and so can't defend himself.

Six

AT SCHOOL THE TEACHERS used to send me to town regularly. I was fast and, as my father discovered from his horse, I was equipped with a jet engine. One day I broke a record by leaving school at 11:20am, going a distance of over four miles and back. When the bell announcing the end of recess rang, I was back at the school. The teachers thought I had lost the money and decided to come back before I reached town. However, I showed them everything I had gone to buy. They asked whether I had got a lift back. I said no. The school principal took me before the school assembly and told all the children at school about my speed.

From then on I was encouraged to become an athlete. But there was never much time for that, especially after my mother passed away. School was a pleasure, the only problem being money, not having enough to buy books and clothes. We used to take turns. Monday I would go to school. Tuesday my brother would go and I would mind the cattle.

One day, while we were swinging on the gate at the entrance of the school, I lost my grip. All I remember is that I saw some stars. The rest I can't remember. When I regained consciousness, it was dark. I was at home sleeping, surrounded by my relatives and neighbours. My mother called me and I replied. She asked if I felt any pain. I said yes, in the arm and leg. She wanted to give me some food but I told her I had no appetite. She tried to spoon feed me a little but I couldn't eat much. I was taken to the doctor the next morning. He did his best and failed. I was then referred to the local medicine man: my grandfather. With the little he knew he tried his level best. But he was only good as a herbalist, and this, what hurt me so, was beyond his powers.

He failed in his treatment. I was taken out of school and sat around doing nothing.

But without warning my grandmother, my mother's mother, came to our homestead. She and my mother took off into the distance, carrying me on their backs. For this, they took turns. They never told me where we were going. By this time, I was used to travelling long distances without a word being uttered as to our destination. But anyway, I was delirious, I even preferred death to the agony I was in. However, as you must have guessed, I didn't die. But that day, strange things happened.

We walked for about six miles, until we came to a big kraal with many huts. At the entrance of this kraal there were a number of bottles hanging about. All of them contained some watery substance. I was still on my mother's back. When we went past the kraal's enclosure, all my pain seemed to disappear in a miraculous way. I even asked my mother to take me off her back. She refused. But after many requests she agreed. I walked into the house.

The house was strange and deserted. The healer was not

at home. We waited patiently for his return. It was dark when he returned. He came back riding a horse. He ordered us to pray. We started praying, and he started praying for the sick. I became frightened. I had noticed that as he prayed for you he would hit you with a shambok. I didn't like it at all. I found this unacceptable, I thought about running away from the whole thing. I stood up, pretending that I was going to pass water – but before I got out of the hut the healer got me with his shambok and started hitting me.

Strangely enough, despite the blows, I never felt any pain. He told my mother that I was trying to run away. He began telling me about my sickness. It was mesmerising: he told us everything about me as if he had a video recording of my life. We spent the night at his house. The next morning the healer demanded that I be left behind. My mother and granny left me. I felt rotten. But what else could I have done? I had to do what my parents told me. So, I stayed at his house, forever homesick.

The only times I enjoyed were times of singing and chanting. I used to like singing a lot. But every time we finished singing I used to think about home and the good meals my mother used to cook. I missed my brothers and my friends. I stayed with the preacher for three months. I got better and went back home. A goat was slaughtered to welcome me. People ate the meat and drank the beer. I was home again safe and sound.

And so it came to pass that I returned to school. Surprisingly, I did very well at the end of the year. I passed and got back into athletics again.

There are many memories which are rushing at me, demanding to be told, but unfortunately I do not have the time to do so. Perhaps one day when we are free from this drudgery I will make the time. But anyway, let me spend some time on aspects that the youth of today might find interesting.

During our times, there were different stages of youth. There were fully grown men (young adults), those that were at the right age for taking wives. Then there were the teenagers, those were chasing after young maids. Then there were the boys looking after the livestock. These age groups never used to mix socially. Let me put it this way, even the elders came in different classes. There were those who were Christians, churchgoers, who wore traditional clothes and the Traditionalists. There were those who wore fine clothes, trying to be 'real' gentlemen, mainly those who went to colleges, teachers and clerks, and those that worked in big cities. These left the 'stick'-life behind ('civilisation' was judged in terms of whether or not one still carried a stick).

Among those who wore clothes there was a group called Izindlavini (those who behaved in an erratic, uncontrolled fashion), they wore big black trousers and white shirts and white caps, and Long-Tom underpants. The trousers were decorated with black and white patches of cloth and a lot of buttons. Even during cold weather they never used to wear overcoats. You would even find them with their shirts in the hand with no tops on come sun come rain. There were days when you would find them wrapped in heavy bedspreads or wearing khaki trousers, with a 40-inch bottom, wielding sticks and a knobkierie. These knobkieries would be stuck into one of the loops and would hang on the side of the body. They used to go in small groups of about three to five, playing mouth organs, and each one of them wore a whistle hanging by a long piece of string around their necks.

There was another group with a similar style. The only

difference would lie in the length of their trousers. Theirs were short, three-quarter trousers. That's how they earned for themselves the name Unozikhindi (meaning short pants).

The last group was called Ntshontshiwe. These groups never used to quarrel. All they did was chase women. A girl would fall in love with a member of the Ndlavini group, then she would leave him and fall for a member of the Short Pants (Unozikhindi). She might get married to him or move on to a member of the Ndlavini group. The people who really disliked each other were the Gentleman and the above three groups. This was because the above three groups used to ill-treat the Gentlemen. Every time a Ndlavini or Unozikhindi met a Gentleman, he would ask him where his fighting sticks were, why he was wearing shoes, and whether he realised he was eroding God's earth. And, as you might have expected, they used to beat these guys up since they did not carry any sticks along.

The people who wore traditional clothing were divided into groups as well. There were the Mashawe, who were well disciplined and lived by their own laws. Among them there was a magistrate, a judge, a prosecutor, a chief, an induna, a policeman, a secretary, a food minister, a chairman, an entertainment officer and an information officer. They did not fight anyone. They only lived for fun.

The second group among those that dressed up in traditional ways were the Nombolas. They used to tease people wearing European (Western) clothes. They would tease them that those clothes made them weaklings, into people unable to defend the area from its enemies.

All this made for a lot of excitement in the social life at my home place. But you could also feel that things were changing fast. People think of the countryside as a place of cows and peace. Yes, both exist and existed but you had to be a daredevil or you would be beaten up to nobody's business.

The only time that was a real pleasure was Christmas time. It was a season that everyone looked forward to. If you had something new, like a new dance or song or a play, you would perform it during the Christmas season, during the Christmas festival.

And it was great because it was the only time all the people could afford to be together because of the migrant labour system.

People came from the factories, the mines and the plantations. Students came from colleges far away. And everybody would return with something new.

I remember one year, the miners came back with a new dancing style learnt from the Bhaca people. Everybody was so excited that they won all the festival prizes. They even came with a new way of dressing, with all of them wearing similar hides. It was really beautiful. Everyone old and young enjoyed it to the fullest. Every aspiring dancer copied it. In no time it was taken up by most of the youngsters in our area and it soon became a local way of dancing.

We learnt the lesson that when you go somewhere you should come back with something new and progressive for the community. Even if you go to school somewhere, you should come back with some knowledge to give to the people. Even if it was something to entertain your local brothers and sisters, it was welcome. So that in the end, although you would find some misunderstanding among the different sectors of our community we all welcomed any progressive act from our fellow brother or sister, no matter whether they were from the Civilised, the Ndlavinis, the Ndombolas or the Unozikhindis.

Seven

AFTER MY MOTHER PASSED AWAY there was no one at home for us to stay with so we had to move to my father's parents. The chief said he would find somebody to look after our home until we were old enough. We decided that we would come home once my older brother was married.

At that time my grandmother was very sick, so there was no one to cook for us. As the only person who could do domestic work, I cooked for everybody and was always late for school. During summer I used to fetch fresh mealies from the field, using a big basket so that I could get enough food for seven people, not counting my older brother. He had run away and found work at Port St Johns.

One day I met my class teacher on my way home from the field. I was carrying a big basket full of mealies and pumpkins on my head.

"Where do you come from, Alfred?" she asked.

"From the fields, Miss."

"What were you doing in the fields, Alfred?"

"Fetching mealies and pumpkins, Miss."

"Who helped you put the basket on your head, Alfred?"

"No one, Miss."

"How did you manage to put a big basket like that on your head, Alfred?"

"When it is half full, I put it on a high bank and fill it while it's there. When I have finished filling it I go under it and pull it on my head. Once it is on my head I won't take it down until I am at home. When I reach home one of the family will help me to take it down."

While she was speaking to me, tears tumbled from her eyes. Then she asked me to stop as she was going to take me halfway. She took the basket, carrying it on her head. For a few seconds she was unbalanced and then we were off. She spoke again.

"Is it nice to stay with your grandparents?"

"No, it's not nice, because I can't do my school work in time. I have a lot of work at home: cooking, getting water from the river, fetching wood to make the fire, and then my school work. I am the one who has to think what the people must eat and then they will be eating while I am on my way to school. I always come home to find that the bucket is empty and that there is no food in the pots. I have to start all over again."

"Haven't you got somewhere else to stay, other than your grandparents' house?"

"No, Miss."

"Where is your older brother? I don't see him at school any more."

"He ran away from home. He wrote me a letter to say he is now working at Port St Johns Hotel."

As I answered her questions she wept more and more. Then she said: "Is this the reason why you are always late for school?"

"Yes, Miss."

"Take your basket. I must turn now."

This time it was my turn to dance with the basket, losing my balance. She stood still for a few seconds – like somebody lost in the big city – then she turned back towards the school. When I arrived at home I was so dizzy I had to sit down for a while. After the dizziness passed, I carried on with my duties. I was late for school again that day, but from then on the principal never punished me. At recess time I was called to a meeting. All the teachers were there and they asked me to tell them all my problems. I cried as I told them and they begged me not to as they were trying to help.

On a later journey from the field with my heavy basket I met a coloured man who owned trucks, Mr Tommy O'Rielly. He was my father's best friend. He asked his work man to load the basket onto the truck and said I must come and sit next to him. He asked me where I came from with that basket. I told him I had come from the fields.

"Are you attending school?"

"Yes."

"Are you not going to be late?"

"I will be late. I am always late because I have to cook first, before I can prepare to go to school."

"Would you like to come and stay with me in town, so you can have enough time to attend school?"

"Yes, I do want to."

"Right. Tomorrow evening I will pass here at 7:30pm. Take your things and wait for me under that big tree. I will pick you up there, okay?"

"Yes, I will do so."

After I was dropped off I went home. The sun took far too long to set, and the night too long to clear for the next day. I was worried about my younger brother, thinking that he might die of hunger. Who would cook for him? I went to school that day and when I arrived back home, my father's sister from Durban was there. She was living at Mkumbane with her husband and three children: Nobelungu, Nontu and Khanyisile. I was very happy, thinking that she would take over the cooking, that I would have time for my school work and for playing stick games with the other boys.

I was very disappointed to find that my auntie's arrival added to the burden on my shoulders. Early one morning I was sitting behind my grandmother, preparing beans for the pot full of stamped mealies on the fire place. My granny asked me to fetch a tin of sugar from the neighbours. I was sorting the rotten beans from the good ones and had to leave this work to ask my granny where the sugar tin was.

As I stood up my auntie drew a piece of burning wood from the fire place and beat me with it, saying, "How are you looking after my mother? You are a cruel child, go to the graveyard and tell your mother to arise and go back to your father's house. I don't want you in this house because you are very cruel."

I ran out of my granny's place, to the graveyard, crying. The place of the grave was just behind my granny's place.

On the way to the graveyard I was stopped by my father's brother's wife, who asked what had happened. I told her the story. She said it wouldn't be a good thing for the people's eyes to see me crying in the graveyard, that it was only two months since my mother had passed away and that this would upset the ancestors. She begged me to go back to granny so she could solve this thing. We returned together. She asked auntie about the story.

"This boy is a liar. How could I say such a thing to my child?" auntie replied.

"No, Makoti, she is the liar," said my grandmother. "It is just as the child has told you."

From my point of view, the time during which I lived at granny's place passed much too slowly; I was very unhappy.

My auntie was a beer drinker. She never went to the field but would leave early in the morning to hunt beer and come back at night, joking and laughing. Once she came in at about 8 o'clock at night, shouting, calling my name and demanding to know what I had cooked. She knew that I could cook. I told her that I had cooked samp with beans.

I told my brother that I was leaving and that I would come back to take him to my new place.

On my last day at granny's place I came back from school. I cooked fresh mealie bread then collected my books and clothes and hid them in the long grass near the big tree. I would hear a truck passing because the road passed close to my granny's place.

Fifteen minutes later I vanished and waited in the long grass near the tree. After 10 minutes the truck came and I said bye-bye to my granny's place. After 15 minutes I was welcomed at O'Rielly's place.

"As from today you are my child," Mrs O'Rielly told me. She called her son, Patrick, and he arrived saying: "I am here, Mummy."

"This is Alfred. He is your brother. Welcome him." We shook hands, smiling at each other.

I was a bit afraid, thinking that I would have to work hard, even harder than at granny's place. Mrs O'Rielly told me what I had to do each and every day. "When you get up in the morning, warm the water, put it in the bucket, go to the kraal and milk three cows. After that clean yourself. Then breakfast will be ready. After breakfast you will leave for school.

"On weekends you have to look after the cows. Every three days you have to clean the cow stable, cut new grass and spread it on the stable. After supper one of you will wash the dishes and the other will wipe them. After all that you do your school duty."

We had supper together and after supper Pat and I washed the dishes. The following morning Pat took me to the kraal and we milked the cows. After that we lit the coal stove – we had to cut the wood with a saw and then chop some with an axe to make small pieces to start the fire.

I enjoyed the new way of working – it was better than at home or at my granny's place. I did not work to be paid, but for Mr O'Rielly to pay my school fees, books and clothing. They gave me about R2.00 pocket money. After a week they went to Kokstad where they bought us new clothing, shoes, briefcases – and new bicycles. It was just like a dream – I had never imagined myself on a bicycle.

Every day I passed my granny's place on my bicycle, coming from and going to school, but I didn't stop. After a month my older brother came and took my younger brother to Port St Johns to my mother's mother.

In 1953 my granny passed away and my auntie came to Mr O'Rielly to tell them that I should go home for my granny's funeral. I was released.

I was at my granny's for four day and then went back to the O'Riellys until I finished my standard six. Mr O'Rielly asked me what kind of training I would like to do. There was carpentry, bricklaying, plastering, plumbing and painting. I chose plumbing and applied at Kokstad Vocationary School. So I spent two years at Kokstad doing plumbing theory. When I passed I started looking for a job, unsuccessfully, until my cousin found me one at Carletonville.

When I was away at Carletonville, Pat O'Rielly was sick for a short time and then passed away.

I was very sad to hear the bad news as he was really my brother. The O'Riellys decided to move from Flagstaff – they had lost their only child. They went to Qumbu where Mr O'Rielly lost his wife. Bad things always happen to good people. I don't know why.

I heard that Mr O'Rielly married another woman and had two children. The man who told me didn't give me their address. At last he told me that Mr O'Rielly also passed way, after promising for so long to give me the address and take me to where Mr O'Rielly stayed.

In 1957 my older brother married and we returned again to Flagstaff, where it was just like before; the only difference was that Mummy and Daddy were not home any more. We went to fetch my younger brother, so we were four with my brother's wife, Mamphankome, from the family of Majola at Maliwa location at Flagstaff.

In 1958 my grandfather was sick for a short period. When he passed away it was the end of our grandparents.

Although we came back home I spent most of my time at the O'Riellys. It was a happy family, although they were very strict. There was a shambok in the kitchen and if you did something wrong you would get it easily. There was no difference between my parents and the O'Riellys.

I praise them for what they did for me. If I have even a little education it is because of Mr O'Rielly and his family and I won't forget them. I will remember them all my life.

Eight

ON 3 FEBRUARY 1964 I set foot on a train for the first time. I was going to Carletonville, promised a job plumbing. My cousin, who had found me the job, met me at the station. When we arrived at his place, the people were happy to meet me. I felt at home.

The following morning he went to work. Work started at seven in the morning. I had to wait for the manager, to get his approval to work there and to see whether I was satisfied with the conditions set down by the firm. Minutes ticked away slowly. I was eager to see myself working. In fact, there were also other people waiting for the manager, looking for a job.

At nine o'clock work stopped, but still no manager appeared. It was tea time. It lasted until 9:15. Work resumed.

I was struck by the way work was done there. It was unlike the way we worked back home. People here worked at a very fast pace. Sweat was pouring down their half-naked bodies. They were wearing nothing from the waist up. Some were building houses, others were pouring cement for the foundations. Some were doing the roofing and others were doing the job I was to do, the plumbing.

They worked in a very determined manner. I wandered around all the departments, looking carefully at the work carried out in each one. There was a nasty job where concrete was mixed. The sun was hot. The black workers, from the ground floor to the third, were pushing wheelbarrows filled to the brim along planks that looked unsafe. I felt as if I was dreaming, I was so scared.

Suddenly, a man who was pushing a wheelbarrow fainted. Other workers rushed to him with a water pipe and poured water all over his body. They also used an air pipe. When he came to his senses they took him to a cooler place.

This incident did not affect the way people were working. They were still being hurried as if it wasn't worth noticing. The foreman kept on shouting: "Kom muntus. Mina funa phelisa lo silep today, hay tomorrow wena yiswakhale. Muntus mina funa we vuka ayifika yifalapha msebenzi kamina." (This is 'Fanakalo', roughly meaning: "Come on, Muntus. I want to finish the slab today, not tomorrow, do you hear? Muntus, I want you to wake up, not to come and die here, in my work.")

Then the foreman came to us. We were watching what was happening. He greeted us and asked if we were all looking for a job. Eight of us wanted a job but the rest said they were only looking on. He said those who wanted work should stand to one side. Those who didn't want work must "fakofu" ("be off"). He didn't want anyone hanging around. Eleven hurried away.

After chasing them away he turned to us and inquired whether anyone was Humphrey's cousin. I said, "I am he, Baas."

He said I looked like Humphrey, but added, "You look like a Boesman. Are you a Boesman? Anyway, I am giving you a name: Mooi Klein Boesman. Do you hear?" he said, raising his big hoarse voice.

I agreed immediately that I was his Mooi Klein Boesman. He came to me threateningly, as if he would have hit me had I not answered immediately.

He told us that at 10:15 the 'Makhulu Baas' (the big foreman) would come to see us to find out whether we were suitable for the job. He wished me luck because he sympathised with my cousin being the only Transkeian on the building site. He also told me that my cousin worked well, was respectful and was dedicated to his job. He was one of the few workers who did not use his absence as an opportunity to loaf.

Of course I agreed with everything he said. What troubled me was whether I would be able to work under these harsh conditions.

At 10:15 the manager arrived. Some of those waiting were no longer prepared to work because of the way people were being hurried. They were driven off like a prison span. One by one the manager asked us what kind of job we did. We told him. I produced my documents. He read them. He smiled and said that I should start work that very moment. He then took me to Mr Jacobs, the foreman of the plumbing department.

Mr Jacobs also seemed to be happy with me. He asked me all kinds of questions. I answered him. I worked that day, worked until the end of the week, worked the following week – without being registered by the firm. Not being registered created problems with the people I stayed with. Humphrey stayed in the same room. The other people feared that since I was not registered I would steal their belongings and be off. This troubled my spirit but there was nothing I could do.

I had spotted a car not far from the hostel. I told my cousin that someone I worked with had suggested I share a place at his dormitory. Of course I was telling him a lie.

I took a towel, soap, some toothpaste and other little necessities. My cousin did not try to stop me because he was aware that things were taking a nasty turn in the room. Things were not well at all. I went to work and, ignoring knock-off time, stayed around until dark.

I went to the car. It had seats but no wheels. I slept comfortably for eight days. On the ninth day, at about 03:30 in the morning, I felt as if the car was overturning. I was falling this way and that. I was frightened. I didn't cry, although I was almost in tears.

I nearly called out for help but that would not have been easy. They would have asked me questions, like what was I doing in that car so early in the morning. I searched for a place to escape and after some struggle I managed to open the door. I grabbed my bag with my belongings and ran as fast as I could away from the car. Once I was sure I was far enough from the scene to be safe, I halted. I looked at the car but I could see nothing strange. The car stood motionless in the night, its door open, and silence prevailed.

I was overcome by loneliness. I was alone in a world of strange people and happenings, wandering through the night with no place to stay, away from people and frightened. I went and sat under a tree until daybreak. I found a tap in the morning, washed myself and prepared to go to work. I didn't tell anyone about my night.

At 10:15, after tea time, Mr Stein arrived and said he

wanted to talk to me. He asked me whether I had a pass book and whether I had it with me. I told him I had it. He said he was taking me to register me. Fear returned when we were at the pass office. People were being sent back to the countryside. All the same I kept consoling myself that I was different because I had never parted with my certificates.

We went to the Labour Bureau at office number 7. Mr Stein carried my reference book and I followed behind. One of the Labour Bureau black jacks (municipal police) asked me: "Where is your home?"

"At Flagstaff."

"How many years have you?"

"Twenty-two years, Baba."

"Is it your first time to seek employment?"

"Yes, Baba."

"Do you see these things?" (Pointing to the handcuffs which were tightened on his belt.)

"No, Baba."

"They will go around your wrists and I will be with you until I dump you in your police station in Flagstaff."

"Why, Baba?"

"You say 'Why, Baba?' You are not allowed to put your foot here. I was at Lusikisiki the day before yesterday. Tomorrow I will be at Flagstaff with you. Matanzima wants his people in the Transkei and not in the cities, so you had better go home."

While he was telling me what was going on I was called inside. I jumped inside. Mr Stein went straight to the counter and started up a conversation with a white official there. The two of them talked and talked as I was consoling myself that everything was to be all right. After some time, he called me and asked if I had accommodation. What did this mean? Was 'yes' or 'no' the right answer? I told him the truth. I did not have accommodation and the place I stayed in (the hostel), I stayed in illegally. I did not tell him that I lived in a car. He asked me if I had R2.50 and I told him I did. The official phoned the hostel and the hostel said that I could come. I had made it.

Mr Stein said I must wait for him outside. When I looked at the paper I found that I was registered. I was so happy that I took my papers to the black jack, saying the official said he must take me home to the Transkei.

He looked at the papers and said, "No, I can't take you home, you are registered. You are lucky, Mfana." After a few minutes Mr Stein came out and we went to the hostel office.

Mr Stein drove me there. They were waiting for us. I filled in their forms and paid my R2.50. Searching through my pockets I realised that I only had 22c left after that. There were three days left before pay day. I was forced to live on 4c a day. I bought 2c worth of bread in the morning and also the same amount for supper.

My room was near my cousin's, I discovered. I went over to fetch my belongings and the people who stayed with him were interested to know where I had found a place to stay. I told them my room was near theirs. They were suspicious and asked how I was able to get this place without being registered. I told them that I was already registered and that I had my receipt slip to prove it. I showed them the card with the number of my bed and the receipt.

"How did you manage to be sorted so soon?" they persisted. I told them that they had to realise that they had wronged me by chasing me away for not being registered. I had come to this place because the white man, the employer, had called me. I had made an application and arrived as a virtually employed person.

They were left disappointed. Having troubled me so much, so hastily, having even threatened to call the police, I was now going to get a room so near to them. They couldn't do anything; it was clear to them too, they had been evil.

Three elderly men showed me my new place of residence. I was by far the youngest. They were glad to have me there. Since I was there, they said, I was to be their errand boy. They were good company and guided me correctly in the ways of that world. One came from Maputo, one from Mzimkhulu and one from Ntabankulu. I conducted myself well and did everything with determination. I was always the first to arrive from work. By the time they arrived I'd already cooked for all, and boiled water for bathing. You see, there were only cold showers.

I worked well on the construction sites – with the same determination. I worked quite happily. Soon I became used to the job and found no problems. But then I got injured.

It was on a Sunday at about 1:45pm. I was on my way back to the hostel from church when I came across three people. All I held was a hymn book and a lotus cane (walking stick) but they assaulted me. I hadn't done anything to them. I could not do anything to stop them. I blindly resisted but they beat me. It was a hard fight. It's difficult to explain how I defended myself from my assailants. Everything blurs in my memory – I only remember pain and confusion.

In the end I found myself lying down in a concrete water furrow. Water flowed in it and stopped and flowed again. There was a bayonet in my hand. Where did I get it from? A policeman arrived on the scene but I did not realise who he was. I kept on fighting. I was put in the back of the police van. It was then that I realised I had been shot in my left leg; my body was blue right round. I had been hit very badly but I never stopped fighting – even inside the van, fighting anyone I could. The policeman drove away. One policeman came and sat at the back with us. We arrived at the police station. No statements were taken; we were driven straight to the hospital instead.

We were admitted and received treatment. I got a few stitches and the bullet was removed from my leg. I was feeling very sick all along, in really deep pain. My friends came to visit me; my boss came with my cousin and asked how I got injured. I told them everything. Even the police came in to ask me to make a statement.

After a week my girlfriend, Sindiswa, came to the hospital to visit me. It was only one month since we started going out, and only two months since she started living in Carletonville. When I proposed to her she had told me that she was going out with some guy I didn't know, but mentioned that she didn't really love him. She said she was just a victim of circumstances, since she was forced to go out with him in order to get accommodation as she had lost her auntie's address. The man had left work and joined a gang called the Russians. He looked older than her father, she told me. Sindiswa came from Mount Frere in the Transkei. She had heard from the guys I worked with that I was in hospital. When she came to see me I was still in a bad state of health, although I looked much better than when I was first admitted.

She told me that the guy who tried to kill me was her

ex-boyfriend. She started crying. I felt so sorry for her that I cried myself. I told her to look around the hospital since all the guys who had attacked me were also lying with me in hospital. She went out for a short time and came back to inform me that one of the guys was in fact the culprit.

I started feeling ill at ease. I couldn't believe that a man could kill me just like that. After some days, when I felt much better, I was able to take a pair of crutches and go slowly from ward to ward looking for this man. I found him lying down, being examined by a doctor. Something inside me snapped and I just wanted to tear him to pieces.

You see I was furious: my kinsfolk were writing to ask me for money for their children's books, and this guy had put me out of work. Lying helpless in hospital was frustrating: where the hell was I supposed to get that kind of money from?

I dropped one crutch down, and as he was lying down there with the doctor looking after him, I lifted the other one up in the air and hit him on the head. Then there was chaos; the whole ward was gripped by panic, patients were jumping all over the place and I kept on hitting. Everyone started to run away. The nurses were the first to disappear – within seconds. But the doctor returned and tripped me with a flying tackle.

I landed with a thud on the floor, unable to stand up again. I sat there crouched, furious and shouting, partly from fear but also from pain, because I had over-exerted myself. I was taken back to my ward.

The hospital staff descended on me and placed my leg in traction. Despite my pain, though, I felt quite happy inside. He had to be stitched all over again after the cuts I gave him on his head with my flying crutch. They could put me in jail, I thought to myself then, and I would not mind.

But I was taken aback when one of the doctors came to tell me that an ambulance was waiting for me outside. And that it was there to take me to the prison. The doctor said that I was to spend my nights in prison because I was such a troublemaker, but that I had to return to the hospital by 9 o'clock every morning for treatment. How I got there was my business, the doctor added. The ambulance took me to my hostel instead. But sure enough, the police were waiting there and took statements from me. After that they left me alone. All my room and block mates came to see me.

I told them everything, and I related to them all my troubles. Some sympathised with me but many argued that I got what I deserved. I also told them I was chased away from the hospital. Some blamed me, others agreed with what I had done. I was, to tell the truth, scared of going to jail.

I was discharged and went back to work. I worked for only two days before I had to appear in court. I felt disgruntled and could not sit down before finding some 'muti' (medicine) for my case. Fortunately one of my roommates in the hostel was a nyanga (a muti man). He administered some muti for me so my confidence increased at court.

I was cross-examined at court. They insisted that the most serious mistake in my actions was to fight another patient at hospital. I told them that I had to; I told them I was forced by circumstances, that I was frustrated, that I was not working because of these people who just decided to attack me.

For four days I appeared in court trying to defend myself and explain my behaviour. On the fifth day the court discovered that two of the men had criminal records for housebreaking and robbery. Still I was accused of taking the law into my own hands by attacking this man, especially in hospital. I tried to plead mitigation: I told the court again that I was out of work because of them, that I could not buy food for my family and that my brother needed school books, that I couldn't take it. I also told the court that it was self-defence and I was well brought up to avoid violence. I respected other people.

Before sentence was passed I was told by the court that I had done them a big favour by exposing these criminals. The magistrate added that my fighting spirit must have been a gift from God (since I was a churchgoer) and that I was brave since they were so well armed. He added that I was lucky I was only shot once; they could have shot me more because they had lots of bullets. Policemen in the area were afraid of these criminals.

The court did not find me guilty. "But," added the magistrate, "you must never make this mistake again. A hospital is a quiet place with all different kinds of patients wanting their peace. Do you get me?"

"Yes, my Lord," I said, trembling in anticipation. I could not believe the magistrate's statement: "The court does not find you guilty."

It was my turn to join the audience and watch Moyeletsi, Sindiswa's ex-boyfriend, the criminal, be sentenced to two years – for possessing a gun illegally and for shooting Alfred Temba Qabula. The court mentioned another three people who had been shot with the same gun.

"The court," said the magistrate, "is giving you a heavy sentence because you are dangerous to this society."

Mjwara, his accomplice, did not have any other criminal records.

Court: "Mjwara, what made you join the gang?"

Mjwara: "I was on a drinking spree and I saw these men wearing 'Russian' uniform. They were well armed. I was terrified so I had to join them! One of them told me that I had to pay a membership fee, buy a uniform and attend meetings. I was trying to defend myself."

He was sentenced to fourteen months' imprisonment; it was his first criminal offence and he was still going to be a state witness in other cases. I was glad, assured of at least two years of peace.

I was glad too that one of my roommates was a witchdoctor. This made me really believe in witchcraft! His muti was so good that even my enemies at court had to agree with me throughout the case!

Nine

I DECIDED TO GO BACK TO WORK and everything went well as time rolled on. We were allowed annual leave in the plumbing department. I took my leave on 20 December, wanting to spend Christmas at home. My friends and brothers in the hostel gave me R120 for provisions and my witchdoctor gave me more medicine. They liked me very much. They were grateful that I used to clean our room, cook and run errands.

They even bought me a second class return ticket. Kloza, my witchdoctor, gave me muti which was in a small bottle. He said: "My son, this medicine is very important. Don't propose love to a woman; tell her that you would like to see her at such and such a place, open this bottle and call the woman by her name."

Before I could even say "thank you", tears were running down my face.

At Pietermaritzburg I waited for a Kokstad train. I arrived in Kokstad the following day and I took a bus to Port St Johns. I was home by 3 o'clock; my relatives were waiting for me at the station.

It was Christmas; everybody was happy, singing, rehearsing for the Christmas Day concert. I was particularly attracted to a teacher from the local school. I told her that I wanted to see her at 9:30 the following evening. She didn't want to talk to me, she said, she was tired and needed a rest. Anyway, at 9:30 the following evening I waited for this woman. I opened my small bottle and after I called out her name, I said: "I am here, come immediately." I closed it and put it back into my pocket.

After about 20 minutes I saw her coming out of her room. I couldn't believe my eyes. She sat next to me and put her head on my shoulder. After 15 minutes she went back to her room. She came back again with a blanket and we sat there until 3:45am. We were in love; I could feel it. I said "Thank you" to Kloza's medicine. In the affairs of love, Kloza's medicine never let me down from that day on.

But before long I decided to leave Carletonville and seek employment nearer home. I did not regret leaving that place of suffering, with its compounds, its violence, its homosexuality, a place crawling with the spirits of unappeased dead miners and workers. The place of gold, dagga, drink and oppression. Yes, the compound, that "small gateway" to "heaven".

The Small Gateway to Heaven

Tall brown walls crowned
    with barbed wire fences
Walls that hide what lives inside
    from all outsiders.
And inside them, the inmates never see
    the world outside

> They hear sounds
> Rumours of lives
> They hear stories.

And on these walls: two gates.
   A small and a big gate
   Just as it was told in the
      histories of custody
   But also in the stories of the entrances to Heaven.

And they feel that they are blessed,
Those elected to enter feel they are blessed
   entering the small gateway to the hostel or the compound.
Those unmarked, those without numbers on their wrists
   cannot enter.
But I entered, I was elected to enter the small gates
And these eyes have seen wonders:
I saw the people sleeping stacked in shelves
   like goods in a human supermarket.

I saw the elect, long strings of men
   in queues
One after the other tracing their steps through
   the kitchens
To meet the sight of men perspiring rivers on their bodies
   of glass
Beads of sweat pouring
   as they were stirring cauldrons of stiff porridge
Stirring away with enormous logs
   and others with ladles shovelling the porridge
   onto dishes made hard like the rockface

And you imagined the heat of your food
    before you received it cold.

Then there were others: with his enormous ukhezo
Fishing for pieces of meat and gravy
Slapping it onto the plate shouting
    to move on, stop wasting his time,
Pouring out insults
Swearing and throwing the plate so the gravy
Poured and smudged surfaces, fingers, anger.

He was having his fun
His daily amusement
    on the brink of a riot.

And at night another is busy courting
    his workmate
Praising him as the beautiful one from KwaTeba
    the one with short breasts saying –
Since you left your sister behind
Please take her place in my bunk tonight.
And he asks and asks him to acknowledge his proposal.

This is the small gateway to Heaven,
    for the elect
For the old men turned to animals
And the young mesmerised by the promises.

And I remember:
When the recruiters invaded our homes
    to get us to work the mines

They would say:
"Come to Malamulela
   at Mlamlankuzi with its hills and valleys
There are mountains of meat
There a man's teeth become loose from endless chewing
And there where the walls are grumbling
Where the stoneface is singing
Promising bridewealth and merriment
There sorrows disappear at the wink of an eye
Come to the place of the
      Hairy-jaw
        where starvation is not known."

And we joined the queues through the small gate to Heaven.
And we found the walls of our custody
   and degradation
   and of work darkness to darkness
      with heavy shoes burdening our feet
      with worry
For nothing
At the place of the Hairy-jaw
   away from our loved ones.

And I have seen this prison of a Heaven
This kraal which encircles the slaves.

And I saw it as the heart of our oppression
And I saw the walls that separate us
      from a life of love.

I felt I would never survive the world of Carletonville, its harshness but also its great distance from my home. As many people from Pondoland have been settled in Natal to work for sugarcane or to work in town in Durban, I decided to look for a job in Natal. My uncle got me a job in one of the firms in Durban. I worked for La Lucia Homes Construction at Mount Edgecombe.

I enjoyed working for this company. I was quite satisfied with my work, and I gained a lot of experience. I was glad to be away from the Witwatersrand and its hostels. My uncle allowed me to occupy a room at his place out at Amauti in Inanda, and although transport was difficult to and from Durban, at least there was kindness and understanding at home.

In 1966 my supervisor, a Mr Crowie, left this company and started his own, and lured me away by promising me a better wage. I left La Lucia Homes in 1966 and joined "General Plumbers", his company which operated from the Red Hill of Durban. Coloured and whites didn't like me but I tried very hard to compete with them. I was not at all happy with the salary they gave me. I sat for an exam in 1970 and obtained a very good pass. I thought I was going to get an increase but I was told that the Government was against equal pay for all.

I felt very small; they laughed at me and passed silly remarks, saying: "Alfred teaches us everything but at the end of the week we get more money." I couldn't take it. I was unhappy and frustrated. In 1974 I decided to look for a better paying job. I managed to get myself a job. I wasn't fussy; I was looking for any job.

Little did I know that I was about to enter an enormous factory gateway to Hell. But in the meantime, before all that, came more hardships of the heart.

Ten

SINCE I STARTED WORKING on this testament, the first thing that came into my head was to write about all the events that took place in my life. At least all the events I could remember: about my home and my working life, about my problems, my joys, my crises, my disappointments. About everything, telling no lies and being as honest as I could despite the hurt.

In Durban, with my arrival, I felt I found peace, happiness and, of course, a wife. But I realised there was no more difficult task than finding the right person to marry. As we say, in these drought stricken parts: "There is no river, without a frog." And in my case, I discovered that frogs were made for water as much as water was made for frogs. And I always despised and was frightened of frogs.

I was made to suffer by a beautiful woman – a woman I thought was to be my wife (and she made me think that she thought so too). Don't look at me now: when I first arrived in Natal, I was full of energy, handsome and out to have a good time with women. In the first year I had four girlfriends, but a fifth arrived with whom I fell in love.

At first I tried to accommodate her alongside the others and continue with my life as normal. She found out but brushed it aside saying that she was not in love with my girlfriends, but with me. She even added that I could go to them, she didn't mind, but she would wait for me. Before long, I was incapable of continuing as before and one by one my girlfriends got rid of me.

She somehow managed to quietly win out and I felt so guilty about the treatment I gave her at the beginning of our relationship that I tried to right the wrong by proposing marriage to her. I felt that she had suffered enough. So I sent my people to her home and her kin asked for their lobola. After the usual haggling we agreed on ten head of cattle, but also large pots, rugs and all that jazz.

My kin, myself included, were poor so all this was to be an incredible strain. Her parents wanted most of the cattle as money, but they insisted on four real ones. It was difficult to get the dreaded cattle. At that time most people were very reluctant to give up their cattle, even for good money. And the price of cattle was climbing high. After a lot of running around we found some at Ndwedwe. A message was sent to them to come and inspect their cattle but all of a sudden they declined to come.

Without warning she started clashing with me: that I was ridiculing her, making a fool of her since I had another wife back home in Pondoland. That was a lie. But overnight everything changed and from her caring self she became a vicious tormentor of my feelings. She badmouthed me in public and made me run around in the community explaining myself and trying to get the story straight.

In the midst of all this madness, she discovered she was also pregnant. Our relationship was deteriorating with her trying to assault me, and me trying to avoid the people's ridicule. But she would use every opportunity to verbally attack me, and like an angry wasp to try and sting me, claiming all kinds of double-crossing intentions on my part.

She wanted to go back with me to my rural home to check whether I did or didn't have a wife. By then though I was angry and not ready to cooperate. If my community heard of her suspicions and the doubts about my integrity they would have cooked me. So I refused.

As the period of birth approached she continued arguing and insinuating nasty facts about me. I kept on reminding her that when a woman was pregnant by any of the Miya men, she should not speak like that, because on the day of delivery she would face complications. It happened like that; when the baby was supposed to move downwards, it just moved upwards. There was general panic and she was operated on to save the baby. The doctors gave up any hope that the mother would ever survive. They put the baby in intensive care and managed to save the mother too.

I used to visit her daily at the hospital. I could not see her during the whole first week, but at last I succeeded, after eight days. Her condition was very bad, and to add to all the difficulties her mind was not working properly. When I spoke to her about a particular thing she used to reply with irrelevant gibberish. I tried to show love and determination to her, trying to remove the picture in her mind, influenced by people wanting to make me her enemy. One day I visited, only to find that she was discharged. I had suggested that she should come to my home when she was discharged because there were rituals to be observed and supplications for the baby to prevent it facing problems. But she did not bother.

A day later she had to wake us up at midnight, desperate because the baby had not slept since she took it home. The baby also never stopped crying, but it was rather sluggish by then and it was losing its voice. My uncle asked her then to explain why she had avoided the rituals and supplications. She said that her mother had insisted that it was not necessary to do anything with the baby. And she accused us of wanting to do 'something' to it as a ploy to see it or take it over. My kin were furious about her replies and her flouting of traditions.

My aunt took the baby and handed it over to my uncle. He took the baby and started to move from room to room with the baby in his arms, mumbling and incanting to himself, to the walls, to the air. He beckoned the ancestors of the Miya clan, generation after generation, he chanted their praise-names and implored them to forgive us. That is when I heard the entire poem of our clan.

He then set impepho alight and the herb's scent filled every corner of the house. Exhausted we all went to sleep. As if by miracle the baby slept and woke up calm and continued to do so for the next three months. And throughout that period it remained healthy. On the third month I went out and bought a goat; I put it to knife and offered it to my son. This, in our clan, is called giving the child a blanket. This is the welcome ceremony that marks its introduction to the ancestral chain.

After the passage of this time, we were supposed to be married, either in church or with traditional rituals, or both. But neither her kin nor mine could bring us together: delay followed delay and another trying and painful period arrived. My wife-to-be started a new round of accusations about having a wife in the rural areas and how many people were busy confirming such truths.

Swallowing my pride, I conceded that she ought to come home with me to check my credentials.

We became the source of much laughter and lots of gossip. Yet, however much I tried to ignore people's tales, they kept on arriving in my ears and it hurt a lot. Also, people used to come to me and say that I should give her up, because her homestead was run by witchdoctors with suspect intentions. And they insisted that they would find a new partner for me, more suited to my life. But I kept aloof from them too, desperately trying to make our relationship work. Every day I would go to her, only to find her fuming at me, having to spend my time appeasing her.

Things had taken a dramatic turn for the worse since my marriage proposal and the lobola was agreed to. And although each night it seemed that she was appeased and ready to give us a chance, by the next morning she was wearing her boxing-gloves.

The baby was born on 22 November 1967 and by mid-1968 we split. She announced she had another suitor, and that I had to go to get my lobola back from her father's place. And she boasted that her chances were good due to the large family she came from, unlike my situation which was one of being an orphan, single as a finger, and without say over my father's brother.

She said all this to me as if she was reading it from a piece of paper. She left me standing there dumbstruck and my heart drizzling blood from the pain. I worried about leaving behind yet another motherless child – just like me. But I stared: looking at her walking down the path through the sugar cane fields of Bhekani, and crossing the gum-tree forest near the foot of the hills. And then ascending again on the path through more cane fields to disappear from my life.

Long after her disappearance I found myself still standing and staring for no rational reason. She had gone with her bitter crop that she sowed in her heart. And I found myself lost and tired. I sat down in the shade of a gum-tree; the weather was turning cold and the wind, I remember, started rattling the leaves. And the tree seemed to taunt me: I was jilted by the mother of my child. A beautiful child – for whose existence I thanked both God and the ancestors time and again.

I went over the passions I hosted: my fears as she was being cut up, my worries that she was disabled for life, my anxieties that she was to die giving birth. I remembered the death-do-us-part promises and got up and walked home.

On my arrival home I reported the matter to my relatives who refused to believe my story. They asked me what kind of insults I had been heaping upon her to anger her so. I tried to explain to them what had happened but it was difficult. To this day I cannot find the reasons. Had I been nasty to her, she would always have had my uncle's homestead to complain to, or demand that I was put in my place. But nothing of the sort ever happened. I was ditched and for months to come I was listless, getting thinner and developing a scraggy kind of look.

The community started buzzing once again with rumour. The new rumour was that I received a calling from the ancestors to become a sangoma. My diminishing appearance was a result of this calling and everybody inquired how severe the pains were. I attempted in vain to convince them that I was not in that kind of pain and that I was healthy.

One day, on my arrival from work my aunt called me

"Mfana" (as she used to call me), and added that there was something she wanted to discuss after our evening meal. I knew immediately that it affected me somehow but she first prepared the supper and we ate in silence. After our evening prayer she searched her apron and took out a letter and ordered us all around her to listen to it.

The letter was written by the mother of my child; and the letter was full of insults directed against them – swearing at them, calling them animals and telling them that she did not love their "son" to whom they gave birth through their ribs. And as for their grandchild, they could come and take him because she was very busy relating to "top" people in the area, people of substance, not rubbishes and nothings like us.

I cannot include all that she had written here. I do not like to reproduce all the insults; they are shameful. On the following weekend we sent people to go and inquire the aims of the letter written by my girlfriend. Our people returned immediately saying that she was extremely rude to them and she was not ready to communicate with anyone.

On the following Wednesday I got a summons calling me to appear at the Verulam court. I went there and found her waiting for me. We were three when we entered the court. Us two and the baby. The clerk there asked whether I knew the lady.

I confirmed that she was the mother of my child. His second question was why I shirked the responsibility of maintaining them. I told him that that was a difficult question to answer because the situation was not of my making. I was expecting to marry her and maintain her but they turned me down. He then inquired whether I had paid lobola and I told him that I paid everything they had requested. Cattle and all. He then turned to her and inquired whether I was telling the truth. She conceded that I was.

"Then will you be marrying this person?" he asked. And she said no, she did not love me any more and that she had got advice from home to avoid such a marriage. She was to marry someone from Swaziland instead.

The clerk then said that this issue was becoming too big for his authority and ordered us through another door. He took all his notes, from our statements and took them to the assistant magistrate. He described everything to the magistrate, and the magistrate in turn re-asked us all the questions. After that I produced all the receipts of my lobola expenditure totalling R2 100. The magistrate wrote further summonses calling all the in-laws to court. Tempers were flaring when we all met the next Wednesday in court.

One of the sources of anger was that the child kept running to me in court and trying to play with me. She got cross and tried to prohibit it, but it cried and cried until it got its way. The child kept close to me for most of the court-case.

The assistant magistrate questioned my 'father-in-law' first: he called me the husband of his elder daughter. The magistrate tried to clarify: husband or boyfriend? He meant a real husband because I had paid the lobola and the only deed outstanding was for him to go and inspect the live cattle I had bought.

The magistrate then inquired whether I had called him to see these heads of cattle. He admitted that I had. But he did not do so because he did not get an opportunity to do so. And had I in earnest asked for such a marriage, he inquired. The answer was affirmative: I had done so even before the birth of the child. So why did he not deliver his side of the responsibilities to seal the wedding? He replied that he did not get the time due to his job.

The magistrate, rather irritated, started enquiring into the inconsistencies of his story: he asked whether he knew that his daughter left me for another man.

When he said that he had heard of some such like talk at home, the magistrate asked why he had then sent his daughter to claim maintenance. He denied that he had done so. Yet she said he did.

As a consequence the magistrate was angered and concluded that: "I shall not demand your daughter to marry with this guy now, but I shall force you to pay back all the expenses he paid to you. He is only to pay for the baby. After that he can pay the maintenance of the baby until she is old enough to go to her father's home."

After this verdict her father changed his song completely and pleaded that he could not afford to pay me back because, as he said, the money he earned from the "Mohamedans" he was working for was little. He insisted on signing the marriage papers there and then. That is when she interrupted and argued that she was not to marry me under any circumstances. There would be no peace in our marriage and she was afraid that I was to avenge her for her stinging words and for the troubles she caused.

I was also asked to comment: I stressed that I was always fond of her but after her stinging insults to my parents, after her rejection I could not see how we could live together in the same homestead.

Finally the judge reprimanded her father for not honouring his commitments. He then gave us time to come up with a settlement that involved my compensation. My 'father-in-law' (who was not to be that) was cross: he got into the company car he was using and screeched away into the distance, alone.

The child and both of us parents rode the bus to Amauti. But after the bus ride the child would not leave me. So I accompanied them all the way home. Still she would not let me leave. The neighbours started gossiping about this but it had to be separated from me for the time being, however painful.

Over the weekend the whole family gathered to discuss the issue. We agreed that I wouldn't take anything from my wife's family. But, we decided, we would only let them bring the child up until she reached the stage when she would want to come home.

On that score the settlement was achieved: they wouldn't claim maintenance for the child and I would have a right to see the child anytime. If she wanted to come home she could and if I wanted to do anything for her, I could. The child's mother never married the other guy either, and in later years our child joined my family. We still greet each other when we meet and the years have made the pains disappear.

I then decided not to get married because I had tried to do what I was supposed to do but could not succeed. I couldn't trust women any more. I felt they are very good at robbing and pretending that they are in love when they are not. I told myself that I must work and keep my money as I had done before and forget about women. They are the crocks of love; they are beautiful for nothing.

I stayed alone for six months. Then, one night I dreamed of my mother. In my dream I was at home in Flagstaff where I was born and grew up.

We were at home with my brothers: my elder brother Vuyisile and younger brother Mtu, and my uncle Ernest. My mother had cooked very nice food for us that day and she started dishing it up. She served my uncle first and then herself, my elder brother and my younger brother. I was the last to be given food by my mother.

After I had thanked her for giving me food she said, "Eat and be strong. I want you to grow up to be a big man. Be wise; think before you do things.

"I know that the Mcanyane family has done wrong to you and you are angry for that. I want you to get a place for yourself, a home, so that when I come to visit you I will know where to find you. Even myself, I am very upset about this. But I must know where to visit you when I remember you."

I woke up. Oh! Was I dreaming? I started to think back to my dream. I was very happy about my mother's visit. I wished she would come again. The whole day I was singing and the other workers asked what was happening to me. Why was I so happy? When I told them about my mother's visit they just laughed at me.

Slowly it came to my mind what my mother meant by saying I had to get a place where she could find me when she remembered me. But that did not change my mind to think of getting married again.

The year went on. On Good Friday 1969 I dreamed again. There was a sister born after me who passed away soon after her birth. You could say I had only heard about her because I was too young when she was born for me to remember or for me to recognise her now. But that night in my dream she was a person I knew; she was my little sister. She came with a lady I had known a long time ago, by the name of Nellie Nqunqa. We all grew up in the same area although Nellie was younger than me and I was in love with her uncle's daughter. I used to call her 'sister-in-law' but her sister left me and married somebody else. I respected her very much, just like a real sister-in-law.

In my dream I asked my sister where she got my sister-in-law. But she did not answer my question. Instead she asked me a question: "Is she your sister-in-law?"

I answered her: "Yes, but I was unloved by her uncle's daughter."

My sister said: "She is the one who is going to build us a home. You have to go home to get her."

I woke up and started to think that I was dreaming again.

At that time my girlfriend was busy with a new boyfriend, always passing nearby my home, showing off. I proposed love to one girl, Janeth, of the Mazibuko clan who was my girlfriend's neighbour. I won her love. I used to pass my girlfriend's home. The whole family used to come out to the house and watch us walking slowly by. Sometimes we would stand under a tree in the shade for a long time. Sometimes she would walk half way with me, then we would stand for another hour, then I would take her back half way again before we could leave each other.

After some time my old girlfriend went to my new girlfriend and shouted at her, asking why she was in love with me while she knew that I was the father of her child.

Janeth answered: "I love him because you failed to love him. So do not worry about him, he is mine now. I will shut your big mouth with a stick if you come and talk about him again."

We pushed our love very much. But even though Janeth

loved me so much, there was a thing which was ringing in my mind: do not trust a woman, women have not got real love, they always pretend. The other thing that warned me was my sister's dream, which sometimes came three times a week, saying the same words: "She is not your sister-in-law. She is the one who will build a home for us. You will go back home to fetch her."

So her dream became my daily bread while I did not want to get married. One day Janeth came to me and said: "I want to tell you something. I know that you are not ready to get married. There is somebody who wants to marry me. What must I do? I know that you love me but this man has been worrying me for a year now and some of my family feel I should marry him. If you say I must marry him I will do so, but if you say I must not I will not. I love you, Alfred, and I am still prepared to love you if you want me to do so."

I said to her: "Yes, Janeth, I love you. You know that I love you but I stop you from going on to build your future. I thank you very much for the time you spent with me and also for telling me the truth of what is in your mind. I am still confused but I do not want to confuse you. I wish you all the best. The respect you gave me, double it to your husband. You know what Mavis has done to me. You must not do that to your husband, Janeth. Please."

It was our last day together. After a week, pushed by my sister's dream, I decided to visit the Transkei. I told Uncle and Auntie that I wanted to go to Flagstaff to see the people. On Friday, after I had finished work, I took a bus to the Transkei.

I was in a hurry to be in Flagstaff, to see if Nellie was still around, not married. We left Durban at 6pm. I was in

Flagstaff at 12pm. When I went home there was great joy at seeing me but some people asked if I was sick. I said: "No, I am well." But I was thin like a sick person.

I started to ask people about Nellie: "Is she still around, not married?" They said she was not married and I slept well that night. The following day I went to see her, meeting her on her way to fetch water from the river. It was very nice to see her. We started to tell stories of long ago, of our good times years back, and criticising the present times. She told me she was going to go to town. I told her I was going to join her. On the way to town I started my story of love, although I did not propose marriage. I hate the idea of proposing marriage to a woman just to catch her. Most men do that, when all they want is love.

Then there was a big battle between the two of us. She told me that it was impossible for her because her people were going to say that she was taking her sister's man and because she took me as her brother. She said I knew that I was the one who had always sent her to my other girls, that she had helped me propose love to other girls. That was the truth. It was a long battle, until I returned to work. After that there were letters carrying proposals from my side to her side and from her side to mine for about three months. Then we came to an agreement. I was very happy.

After I met her it was the end of the dream about my sister. After six months in love with Nellie, I changed my statement to her. Early in 1970 I visited Nellie with a new idea: that I wanted to marry her. But she would not believe me – so it was another battle again. She told me that she did not want to marry me because of her mother.

Nellie is her mother's only daughter. In fact there are two children, but with different mothers. Her older brother was born of her father's first wife who ran away because he did not support her. When he was away at work he used to forget that there were people in the rural areas who he was supposed to maintain. So his first wife left Nellie's older brother to the family. After some years her father came back and married Nellie's mother, while she was pregnant.

When Nellie's father passed away she was brought up by her mother. She did not want to marry because she wanted to be able to look after her mother. But after I worked hard to make her understand that I was preparing for her future, she agreed at last.

Again I sent the people to her parents and I started paying lobola. In 1971 her family told us that we must prepare for the marriage. The whole of 1971 I worked hard to get all that we would need for the marriage. During the last three weeks of December our names were called in church – so that anybody who opposed our marriage could come up with their problems before the marriage took place. No one came forward – so on 2 January 1972 we were married.

It was a great day. Neither of us will ever forget the hundreds of people who were there to see us stepping to a new life. It was her first day of getting a new person to rely on, other than her mother who brought her up, and who gave her everything.

On 3 March 1973, our first born, Noduma, was born. She was followed by Msawenkosi in April 1975 and Nokukhanya in August 1977. That is how I came to be a married man and a father of three.

Eleven

IN 1974, ON 6 JUNE I LEFT MY JOB at General Plumbers and joined Dunlop. I was fed up with doing skilled work for nothing. I felt cheated, exploited and angry.

The first thing I was asked to do was to fill in forms. These pieces of paper asked where I was born, my last standard at school, where I started work, why I left other places I had worked, and in these papers there was a trick question: "If you are requested to work overtime, will you agree or refuse?" You could say nothing but 'yes' – if you said 'no' you had no chance of being employed at Dunlop.

While all this was happening we were cautioned to watch out for Dunlop's resident doctor who made people fail their tests at the drop of a hat. If this happened, you would be diagnosed as unfit for work.

We saw this horrifying doctor on 7 June. One of us was so afraid that even the doctor noticed and asked him why he was trembling. The male nurse (who was also black) was quick with an answer: he explained that the man was troubled because he had received a message in the morning that his niece had passed away. All 12 of us were hired that day.

On 8 June we went to the chest clinic and were certified in good health. It was only then that we stopped being afraid. On 9 June we were given overalls and in our new uniforms we were sent to 'school' to be taught the rules of the firm and its history.

Our teacher told us how John Boyde Dunlop was a veteran doctor when he saw his son coming from school riding a bicycle which was in a bad state. This pained him a lot and he began to think of a way to improve the tyres on his son's bicycle. He immediately went to the rubber manufacturers to ask them if they could make something to put on his son's tyres so that the bicycle could travel smoothly on the road. They sat down and made the bicycle tyre. It was then that the Dunlop Company was formed, in Birmingham London. It spread to South Africa and is spreading still.

Duma, Langa and the writer of these pages were singled out and taught to drive the Hyster – the forklift. We were told that we would work on a three shift per day, 17 shift per week system. Little did we know that the 17 shift system caused the 1974 Dunlop strike, which caused dismissals, which caused the vacancies for our employment. The shift system plus the company's wage policies had incensed the workers.

Before 1974 there was a 15 shift system. People demanded higher wages because the cost of living was rising fast. Dunlop said all right, but then we have to get 17 shifts out of a working week. In the old system shifts were from 6am to 2pm, 2pm to 10pm and 10pm until 6am. Working on Saturdays was overtime and paid as such. Workers would average 37 hours of work per week plus the Saturday. With the extra two shifts, work would start on Sunday evening, making people work 45 hours before overtime. So the wage increases were not really increases at all.

The 1974 strike happened because the workers did not want the 17 shift system. In the mill department the whole shift was dismissed and we were employed to replace them. We were hired as scabs. At first we didn't know that the section leader of our department was in hospital. The striking workers had almost killed him because he went to work. They caught him outside Dalton Road hostel. He spent many months in hospital.

I will never forget what the other drivers did to me. They claimed that we had come to rob them of their jobs (ukubephuca umbele emlonyeni). They had been working overtime (from 6am to 6pm), receiving a lot of money, and our employment threatened their overtime. Some of them did not give us proper training.

One day my brother Langa was trying to drive the forklift but it ran down an embankment. Not used to driving a car, he stepped on the clutch instead of the brake. He could not control the steering wheel and the truck went right down onto the dangerous rail ramp, hitting a big wall inside the factory. Fortunately, Langa escaped unhurt. Afraid that he would be fired, we advised him to say that he was too short to reach the brake and clutch. We put pillows in the driver's seat to bring him closer to the steering wheel. When the inspector came, he exonerated Langa because he saw the pillows and saw that Langa was driving well.

People repeatedly threatened that I would not work for long at Dunlop. I told myself that whatever happened I would be patient and prove them wrong. I survived their taunts and threats until, after a long time, I was accepted.

I worked on the forklift, feeding the milling department's machines with chemicals and raw materials to make rubber. I would spend my days and nights driving from the base stores to the mill and back.

That place is hell: all the workers there are pitch black from the black dust and powder that pollutes the place. I was pained by the way people were exposed to such harmful powders. Some had plastics over their overalls and wore masks on their faces. I remember Mr G. Mbele who, after weighing a chemical, needed to go and bathe his body and throw away his overalls. There was another wool-like substance which also produced the need to have a bath after you had weighed it.

It is said that people who worked in these departments were once given milk rations. But these were stopped as it was claimed they cost Dunlop lots of money. A person works under difficult conditions at Dunlop. He works for one day on a job meant to take two days.

When we arrived we were shown around this weird jungle of machines spinning and clanking away: "This is Banbury No 1, Banbury No 2, this is a storage compound for Banbury No 3, which grades the final compound, the stage compound Banbury No 4 grades stage C which goes down to pour out the rubber to the mills, which go to pipes which have water with soap so that the rubbers do not stick to each other. These rubbers enter through the conveyor belt. These rubber stacks are 2 ft 6 ins wide. It depends on how the mill man has taken it out; he is the guide boy. At times the rubber is a long stack; at times it comes out in pieces which are separated by plastic so it does not stick together."

There, on my forklift, most of the time isolated from the world, I would spend my working hours composing songs about our situation. I suppose this was my little resistance struggle in my head, zooming up and down to the Baser Stores and back. When the tunes rolled fast I would work like a maniac, driving my co-workers insane because the materials would pile up fast in front of them. When the songs were slower I suppose life improved for them.

But there in my head, those forests …

They still lingered on in my memory – the only refuge from my father's beatings, my hunting ground which used to provide me with all kinds of birds, my prey, before I turned into prey for others, the hunted.

I remembered how the honey bird was for us the most sacred of the birds. With uncanny accuracy it led one to the beehive. The only reward it sought was a piece of honey cake. To the ungrateful and greedy it retaliated just as swiftly – it led them with the same accuracy straight into a venomous snake or a wild animal.

The forest was its own universe full of wild fruit and dangers: mambas and crawling creatures of all kinds.

Always a source of refuge for the homeless and the frightened, I remembered how during the Mpondo resistance it housed the Congress fugitives. It hid away teachers and commoners; it covered their tracks. But policemen and soldiers would also enter and ransack its goods.

It was a retreat from the wilderness of the world outside: the harsh world of beatings and torture and interrogations; the so-called normal world marked with murderous lists of names.

A source of fear but a source of awe and admiration.

The honey bird was effective in demonstrating its dissatisfaction. It refused to work for nothing. It demanded its just reward. This was also our position as toilers; we left for the forest when we refused to surrender our land, when we rejected the rule of the chiefs who sold our land without consulting us. But we were less successful that time.

When MAWU got entry at Dunlop I knew that the march through the forests had restarted. The Dunlop officials knew that they had to respect their workers, that they had to pay their workers an adequate wage, and that the voice of the workers would not be muffled. But they continued in their old and cruel ways.

In the Tracks of our Train

We assembled its pieces together
    and it grumbled and roared.
Its grumbling and churning
    has caused unrest
    in the stomachs of the capitalists.
They shout from the top in Pretoria:
"But what IS happening?"

There was no answer from Pretoria's hills
    but the Drakensberg mountains
    and the plains of Ulundi shook.
And they said there:
"Yes, this engine is powerful
    and it raises great flames and much uproar
It was ignited on purpose
    to choke us
    and punish us with fumes and heat."

God created bees
    and they produced sweet honey
    and the people praised God for the bees and their honey.

Satan was angered again
> so he created flies to destroy the honey of the bees
>> and the flies sprayed and relieved themselves on it
>> and the people were angered by Satan and his flies.

Satan said: I know, I know.
> Typical.
Everything done by me is never praised
> it is always criticised and scolded.

What we have made moves forward
When its wheels wear out, our unity jolts it forward
When they block it on its way to Cape Town
> it does not lose its power, it roars ahead.
When they block it on the road to Johannesburg
> it does not lose its power, it roars ahead
> it grumbles on, with flames and fumes and anger.

But they gossip and plot out its undoing
> and they accuse its anger of a communist plot
> and its roar of subversion.

And we follow its tracks, also singing.

The powerful ask:
Who allowed these stalks of cane, these blades of grass
> to sing?
Songs are the property of trees, you have to be tall
> you have to have stature, substance and trunk to sing
But we sing
Many with eyes get confused by the stature of trees
But at least our song reaches the blind.

They listen to it closely
    and understand
That the deals their capitalist suitors
    have struck up at the Sopaki grounds
    might feel like bangles of gold
    but they rattle like chains.

Across the river the grumble is heard
There is motion and uproar
The people will it to cross the waters now:
    To jive and to dance on new grounds
To hum more pleasant sounds.

We agree.

I continued working at Dunlop. The foreman of our section hated me for no reason at all. He always accused me of not listening to instructions, but when I asked him why he could not answer. He would give me work to do and then, after I had done it, would complain that I had not done it properly, that I was very slow, that I had no respect for authority. Then he would threaten to fire me.

One day just before I started work, when I was still reading the programme, he said that I had disorganised his section, that I had delivered half standards and rejects. I called the chief officer to question the foreman about this matter. He repeated what he had said and the foreman insisted that he would fire me if I continued with my behaviour. The induna came to my rescue.

The section head supported the foreman, accusing the induna of protecting me because we were working together and were very close friends. He said we loved each other as man and wife and he wished to know who was the man and who the wife. The induna was wild. But nothing came of it.

One day I had gone to the store, where we fetched material to make rubber. As I entered the stores, an order slip fell off. I climbed off the forklift to pick it up but the wind blew it away. I ran after it and when I reached it the wind threw it further away. Eventually I caught it. The place where I had parked the forklift was near the platforms where the machines were off-loaded from the railway trucks. When I picked up the order slip, I saw the forklift falling onto the railway lines.

I thought to myself: "I am already fired because I have forgotten to pull the handbrake." Other drivers appeared on the scene and tried to help me formulate a story based on lies.

I refused and told them that I would tell the truth and get fired because I had made a mistake. I went straight to the Internal Transport section to report the event. I proceeded to my milling department and told the section head, who hated me, about the accident. He laughed so loud and his back teeth could be seen.

He said: "I have long told you that you are very irresponsible. Today is your last day here. You are a fired man. Internal Transport is going to fire you before I have done so."

I replied that I knew I would be fired and went back to the scene of the accident. The manager and engineer were there when I returned. They said not a word but the forklift was taken to be repaired. The manager said I would have to wait for the engineer's report, but that he liked the fact that I had told the truth and had not lied.

I knew that there was only one way for me, that there

was no parting of ways, even though the manager had consoled me. I had already told myself that I was fired. Many days elapsed but nothing was ever mentioned about the incident.

In our department we had to buy safety boots. I organised all the forklift drivers of my department to go to the shop manager and demand free safety boots. We went to him three times but heard one story: the company does not give free boots.

"You will get nothing – you will be fired," they said.

"Even if I am fired, I won't mind," I replied.

It was Friday afternoon when I planned this idea. After finishing at work I went and bought myself a pair of sandals. On Monday, instead of wearing boots I wore sandals and started to work. A senior foreman said: "Alfred, you are not supposed to wear sandals in this department, do you follow me?"

"Yes, I follow, but these are all I have."

"Tomorrow you must not come to this department without your safety boots."

"I will because these are the only thing that I have."

The following morning I came in wearing my sandals. He came to me and said, "Alfred, you are still wearing sandals?"

"Yes."

"I do not want to see you in this department."

"Thank you," I said and went to tell the manager my story. He said the senior foreman was right but that he was going to write a requisition so that I could get boots. But, he said, the company was going to deduct the money from my wages slowly.

I said: "No, I do not want my money to be deducted

because I have bought sandals which also let my feet breathe."

He asked me if I signed the book every month. I said yes.

"Why do you think you sign every month?"

"I do not know. I was told to sign and all the workers were signing, so I signed it."

The manager called Khumalo, a member of the liaison council of the department, to explain the law of the company. I told Khumalo that I understood what they were saying, but that my problem was money. And that I was not prepared to buy boots while I still had new sandals. The manager told Khumalo to go back to his work as he was going to sort me out.

Together we took a fast walk to the gate where we met a security guard. Without even saying 'let us go', he just walked off. I followed him. We entered the personnel department where the safety officer was talking to another man. The safety officer asked what had happened.

"You see this man? He is wearing sandals."

"What kind of job is he doing?"

"He is a forklift driver."

"Do you remember what happened last week next to your department? A forklift fell down near the ramp. If that driver was not wearing safety boots he would have lost his feet," said the safety officer. "If he is a driver, give him safety boots."

"You see," replied the manager, "I would give this man boots but tomorrow six men will come and demand safety boots."

"Understand what I say. Even if there are six hundred, if they are drivers, give them safety boots."

The manager did not say thank you or goodbye, he just turned, opened the door and we left together. We walked back to the mill department without talking to each other. We entered his office. He opened his desk drawer, took out his requisition book, wrote the date and asked for my employee number.

"41061."

"What size?"

"8."

"Go to the internal shoe shop and get your boots."

"Thank you," I said and left his office singing, "Amandla ngawethu siyonqoba simunye."

I gave the requisition to the shop man, and he gave me the boots. I tried them on and they were all right. I went to the change room, opened my locker, taking a towel and soap. I cleaned my feet and my sandals. I kissed my sandals and put them in my locker. Then I went back to my old horseback and work.

After lunch the senior foreman came to me praising my boots, saying they were very nice.

"Yes. They are very nice and I just got them for nothing – they are for free." He was very disappointed and I started shouting to the other drivers that they must go to the manager and demand their boots.

"I have opened the closed gates," I said, waving my fist. "It's a victory comrades! We will overcome these employers. Let us be together and fight the evil employers. Amandla!"

All the drivers came and said: "You are very brave. We were afraid, thinking that you would be fired. Forward with our struggle!"

Twelve

Neither the manner in which we were treated nor the working conditions improved. The place was still full of black dust and dust from various chemicals, which make you cough – even if you are not directly involved in that section. My foreman continued to work in the same section, was promoted to senior foreman and became very nasty towards me.

One evening when I was working night shift, just after I had bought a Ford Escort car, he kept on calling me to accuse me of making mistakes. He failed to make me sign for these mistakes but said he had to fire me because I had a lot of money (I was a boss). He did not know why I worked at Dunlop because I drove a lovely car.

We were told one Friday that we had to work from midday on Sunday. I excused myself as I had already made preparations to go home. I went off on Saturday and came back on Monday morning, leaving home at 1am to arrive at work at 5:30am. At 6:30am I was called to the office where I found the foreman cancelling my forms. He took out my card and wrote on it, without speaking to me.

After he had finished what he was doing he told me to 'sign here'. I wanted to know why I should sign. He said, because I had not turned up at work on Sunday. I told him I was not prepared to sign because I had only been told on Friday night that I would be working on Sunday, after I had made preparations to travel home to the rural areas. The counsellor told me that the factory regulations stipulate that if a worker does not turn up for work he has to sign a warning.

I told the counsellor that I would not sign. "I want to be fired by you, here. You know a lot about Dunlop's regulations and you know too much English. Tell them to fire me. I will tell the whole world that I was fired because I refused to work on Sunday. And when I receive my pay I will throw it in the rubbish bin." My enemy (the foreman) stood up and told me that I was ordered to work on Sunday.

"But," I replied, "only on Friday night, when I had already bought a sack of potatoes, a case of tomatoes, meat worth R10, cases of fruit and a sack of oranges. Who was I going to share the food with? I stay alone in Durban. That is why I say you must fire me if I did the wrong thing by not reporting to work."

I then turned my attention to the counsellor and inquired why he had come to the office. He said he had come to hear my case.

"Have you come to persecute or defend me?" I asked him.

"Do you think the counsellor can prevent you from signing and being fired?" the senior foreman asked me.

"Yes," I said. "I have chosen him for that purpose."

"You will never see that happening in this factory."

"Buzz off, you are not my lawyer," I told him.

"He is not going out of this office because he is here to defend the company and not you."

"If he is not here to defend me but the company it's okay, chase me away, because I won't sign."

He then said that it was not a verbal warning, that it had to be signed. I told him I wanted to be chased away because I refused to sign. He became very angry and told me fiercely to get out of his office. "But I will get you one day; I will make you sign; you think you are clever."

I did not care; he could speak and say anything. I knew that he did what he did all because I had bought a car.

One day in 1976 when I was still working at Dunlop a telegram arrived for me at work. It said: "Come home immediately!" Something had gone wrong.

The supervisor gave me the telegram and when I told him I had to go home he went to tell the foreman and the senior foreman. The senior foreman said he wanted me at work, that I was telling him a load of rubbish. I did not bother him but proceeded straight to the Bantu Affairs Commission. They told me to go home but to send a telegram and let them know what had happened and when I would be back.

The senior foreman was very disappointed, claiming that the personnel people were allowing me to go because they were my friends. I asked him why he did not join them and become my friend as well. He answered that I did not help him with anything. I said to him that I would never become a sell out for anybody. He replied that I was swearing at him and that he would have helped me with anything.

At this time conditions were very bad for the workers at Dunlop. They were chased away from work daily.

There was one man, Mr Makhathini, who was liked for

his dedication to work at Dunlop. Trouble started for him when we returned after going home for Good Friday in April 1976. He was getting old, not producing as big a score as before. He was often called and asked whether his still wanted to work at Dunlop. He was made to sign because his production was low, despite the fact that he repeatedly told them that he was not feeling well. Eventually he was admitted to hospital. When he returned to Dunlop he discovered that he had been written off and he was only given money after a long time.

From that time onwards, I hated the Dunlop factory. It used people very hard and then, when they had no strength to produce more, dumped them like rubbish. I realised that I would eventually be in the same position as Mr Makhathini.

I hoped I could do something to protect myself from the cruel hands at Dunlop, because they fired many people who were hurt at work.

I remember one man who was hit by a forklift. He was told to come back daily to sit at the entrance and was given nothing to alleviate his pain. His legs were swollen and he could not even use a stick to walk. I asked him why he did not go to King Edward Hospital. He did and was admitted immediately. On his return he was scolded and fired. There was nothing I could do.

I tried to discuss the bad conditions of work at Dunlop and the manner in which people were fired daily without any reason. One of the workers suggested that we join a trade union. He told me that the offices were at 125 Gale Street. We all agreed to visit the office, to tell them about our working conditions and to ask about the trade union movement.

The forklift drivers decided to meet and discuss what steps we could take to join the union. We were totally dissatisfied with our bonus. Although we produced a lot more than the other workers, our merit bonus was smaller. Through our ceaseless fight we managed to secure a bonus of up to R23 – before this we only received a R2 bonus.

We joined MAWU (Metal and Allied Workers Union) and paid a certain amount every month end. Soon we were organising other workers to join the union.

In 1981 the senior foreman was promoted to shop manager at the Mill Depot. The following Monday he wore a new safari suit and new shoes, limping because the shoes were too tight. I laughed out loud; I could not hold myself in. He became very angry and asked why I was laughing at him.

I told him I was laughing at a conversation I was having with Gumede. Did he want me to laugh at him?

He replied that he was no fool, that he could see I was laughing at him but that it was not the first time a person limped because of tight shoes. If I continued to laugh he would fire me. I told him to fire me because I had not said that his shoes should be too tight for him.

I had already told Gumede that he should say that we were talking about a girl who was walking with her boyfriend. When they came to the Dalton Road hostel, she saw two men playing karate. She jumped very high and kicked her boyfriend on the back so that he fell. The boyfriend was furious and he took his shambok and beat her up. She tried to soothe him by saying: "Oh lovey! Why are you hitting me so hard?" But the boyfriend carried on beating her up.

I told the shop manager that I was laughing at this. He

asked Gumede, who related the same story. The foreman was sorry.

By 1982 many Dunlop workers had joined our trade union. The employers started encouraging people to join their union, the Durban Rubber Industrial Union, which had existed for a long time but had not allowed Africans to join. The DRIU then promised to build all its members high class houses, trying everything to discourage people from joining MAWU as they claimed it was political.

DRIU held a meeting in our canteen. A lot of the workers attended the meeting as it was held early in the morning. But when the workers wanted to know where the union offices were, they discovered that one was in the factory and the other in Pretoria. They wanted to know, if they were fired or had a problem with the factory, how would they enter the factory gates because they would not have a permit to enter? Would we have to wait at the fence and shout to DRIU: "My union! Come, it's me! I have been fired, come and speak on my behalf!"

The reply was: "Yes, you would have to do that." All the workers left the meeting just then. The speaker had already told the workers that they had done the wrong thing by leaving a trade union inside the factory and joining an outside union – MAWU – which would never be given entry.

"So I beg you to join DRIU, a union recognised by the Industrial Council and by your employers. Stop joining a union which will get you fired from work and misuse your money."

Workers left and told them to keep their employers' trade union – they were going to the MAWU meeting. On the same day we went to the MAWU meeting at Bolton

Hall. A lot of the workers, more than 50 per cent, joined on that day. The following week MAWU organisers came to our gates and more workers joined.

One organiser – Mary Anne Cullinan – was arrested by the police. She was taken and brought back three times. Finally they said there was nothing they could do – if she was invited to come she had to come – and they said she must continue with her work.

Finally we held a meeting of all Dunlop workers where we decided that a delegation should be sent to the management to discuss the holding of stop orders. A letter was written and sent to the company. They replied that they were willing to have a meeting at the Royal Hotel and not in the factory. They felt bad that they were going to talk to the workers and not the organisers. I am sure you, the reader of the story, would like to know what was happening inside the factory.

The workers who were in the Steering Committee were just ordinary people who did not dress well and were not well educated. There was a great dispute between MAWU and DRIU. DRIU was saying they had never seen blind people leading each other, that they wanted to see what the outcome of everything would be.

MAWU, on the other hand, was saying: "Leave us alone; even if your spies and informers tell you what they like, we will succeed; we are the leaders."

MAWU members went to the meeting with their organiser, Geoff Schreiner, who management had feared was of East German origin. He was a young man who knew his job well. All members of MAWU were excited; DRIU members were rather sad. When we got the report back from the meeting we encouraged DRIU members to join our trade union organisation because we knew they had made a mistake by joining DRIU. Many of them joined MAWU.

In February 1983, it was agreed that the union could get entry into the factory and in March an agreement was signed. Fifteen shop stewards were elected, three for each department. I was also chosen as one of the shop stewards.

Meetings were held to discuss working conditions and wages. The employers were very reluctant to discuss these matters. This company had not done a good thing for any of its workers but it had done many cruel things.

Some companies help their workers in various matters: they buy them houses and deduct a small amount of money every month. Dunlop claims that they help but only loaned people up to R850. We requested that the amount go up to R2000. After long negotiations, they increased it to R1050. Agreements and contracts had to be signed before you could get the money.

We decided to go slow, so that production was at a minimum, and stopped working overtime. The Minister of Manpower appointed a Conciliation Board to investigate the problems at Dunlop, but it failed to come up with a solution. We started to collect money for our Strike Fund, deciding that we would call a total boycott of work when we were sure everything suited our strike action. At the time there were still a lot of tyres; they were not selling fast because a lot of customers, about 13 per cent, buy their tyres overseas.

We were still seeking a way to overpower the company. A few people were fired and new workers employed but even these were encouraged to join MAWU. We were going to strike when the right time came; we were not in a hurry. Our employers always asked when we were going on strike – they knew we had already set money aside for the strike. We told them that when the time came we would do it, that they should not bother us: "We know what we are doing."

I have never seen such a cruel company. When we started to go slow a lot of workers were fired. The department I worked in was terrible and the various chemicals had a bad effect on the workers' health. People should have been earning more money and receiving a lot of benefits. But none were forthcoming.

I will write more about this bad company. I will not leave it alone yet, as I want to fight for the workers' rights. I hope when you read this story you will note all the bad effects the company has on workers and the gross exploitation which occurs at this firm.

Thirteen

WHILE ALL THIS WAS happening, we had decided to do a stage play of Dunlop workers. This was a play in which the Dunlop workers related their experiences while working at this factory. We performed this play to make our wives and children aware of the conditions of the workplace and the disrespectful way in which we were treated. They had the impression that we were well treated at work, well fed and earned a lot of money which we spent on girl friends.

This play also helped to show other workers the pain and misery we faced at Dunlop. It was highly appreciated by worker communities all over South Africa.

In 1983, when the company refused to respond to our demands, we decided to go on strike. We planned to start the strike on Monday. We were having a general meeting on Saturday, where we were to perform our play on stage for the first time.

Then a lawyer – Mr Cheadle – advised us not to go on strike. We decided we would go back to work and start a go-slow, a canteen boycott, and an overtime boycott. The company had made arrangements because it had spread through the whole factory that the strike was going to happen soon. The company employed many people outside the gate and told them that they must come on Monday when we were going to strike. But on Monday we entered the gate as usual and we began to do our everyday duties.

Then we noticed that there were many people at the gate with their lunchboxes – some with a half-loaf of bread, some with a quarter, some with mahewu. We didn't know what was really happening but the company had employed them to replace us when we went on strike. We carried on with our work.

After three months there was a big rumour (I think it really happened) that the company was sued by the Department of Manpower. The rumour was saying that the company had to pay R68 000 to the Department and to those workers. Some of them had resigned from their jobs because they wanted to work at Dunlop. We often heard people say that the people at Dunlop earn a lot of money. The rumour said that R38 000 was for the Department and the rest divided among those workers, who earned big money for doing nothing – because we didn't go on strike.

After the go-slow, the canteen boycott and the overtime boycott many people were dismissed. We disputed that and the union applied for a Conciliation Board (CB) but the company opposed the CB. Then we just kept quiet and carried on with our work.

In 1984 we started wage negotiations demanding 31 cents across the board but the company offered us six cents. We declared a dispute.

There was a man working at the canteen – the induna – who always teased me, saying: "Hey, you think you're going to win. This is a giant company. This is the government;

you can't overcome this company."

But after we boycotted the canteen a heap of food was dumped. There were high piles taken away and then we dumped some more. We piled a container full of rotten food because the workers didn't buy it any more. This happened until they decided to close the canteen.

We had planned to strike because of wage negotiations. The workers were very angry because the company had taken our yearly bonus, claiming that the company was in a slump because of our stoppages. So we stopped work.

There was a senior shop steward, Baba Khanyile, who came to work at 2 o'clock to find the workers in the canteen, on strike. He came in, just looked at the workers and then changed into his overalls and proceeded to work. We asked the workers what we must do. Where is the senior shop steward? Some workers said: "We saw him going inside the factory, to the department."

Then we sent one of the workers to find him. They found him talking to the managers. He was saying he did not support the strike. Then they came back and reported to us. We asked the workers what we should do. The workers decided to go and fetch him.

I was shocked when I saw him lying on his back; they were carrying him on their shoulders like the comrades carrying their hero on their shoulders on the last day, to the graveside. They dropped him inside the canteen. We asked him why he left us here.

He said: "I was just going to see what was happening inside." So we asked him why he left us without asking what was going on. He was going to work. Then the workers of his constituency said they didn't want him to be a shop steward any more. I am sure he is an Inkatha official

– I know he was a member and after we formed Cosatu he was one of those that didn't come to the Cosatu rally.

After we stopped work the company decided to dismiss us.

At the same time there was the DRIU, which was the company's sweetheart. Most of the coloured and Indian workers refused to join MAWU because they said they couldn't join a political organisation inside the company premises. There were a few coloureds who joined MAWU. But the day we were fired, all of us were fired, even DRIU members. So they decided to join MAWU.

The workers' policy at Dunlop was: if you had refused to join for a long time then you had to stand in the centre of the workforce and tell them that you have repented; that you have come to join the union; that you realise now that it is time to join. They did that and then we gave them joining forms, cards and did everything we had to.

Then we marched out – we were going to build a new Dunlop factory at St Anthony's where we met every day, from Monday to Friday, early – as if we were going to work. We had to report to our shop steward before 7am.

At the same time we elected a group of workers who were going to be our eyes at Dunlop meetings. After a while they came to be known as the 'special boys'. If a person didn't report, the special boys had to fetch him at his home and bring him to St Anthony's by car. One of the special boys had a kombi and we paid for petrol. There were some people who always came with the special boys, who were trying to dive. We warned them that they shouldn't do this because they were trying to break our unity, that we had decided on this strategy to preserve the unity of the workers.

During the first week and the second week there was

no communication between the company and the union. In the third week the personnel manager phoned our organiser to ask him if they could meet at the Royal Hotel. The organiser told him that he had to get a mandate from the workers and that he couldn't come to the Royal Hotel alone. He would have to come with a negotiating team.

The workers gave us a mandate to go to the meeting. We went there and the personnel manager asked if the workers were prepared to come to work. We said: "Yes. The workers haven't got any problem with their work but they want their demands."

They asked if the workers would come back if they respond to the workers' demands. We said: "Yes. They will do so."

That is where we started to negotiate again. They told us that the workers would have to fill in new forms if they came back. They would have to come in as new workers with a new contract and they would lose all their benefits. We said we couldn't accept that but would take it to the workers. They also told us they would suspend 12 workers who were intimidating workers at the company gate.

We said: "No, we can't accept that. We are out for the four people who were dismissed. We can't lose more people." We hadn't done a ballot for the wage negotiations but for the dismissed people – so we stuck to that.

The company hadn't realised that we came out on strike because of the four people – they thought we had forgotten. It had happened in 1983 and it was now 1984.

They made a brief statement and dumped it at St Anthony's. After that the workers said to us, the shop stewards, that we had to stay there with them, that we couldn't go to the company again because the company was not prepared to respond to our demands.

The company phoned the organisers who said the workers had stopped them from coming because the company was not prepared to negotiate faithfully. By the fifth week they called us to negotiate again. We negotiated but came to a deadlock again.

By the seventh week they employed two people from the labour department and gave them R4 each. When they complained that the money was too little the company said it was too much because the job would only take about 30 seconds.

These people came to distribute the pamphlets at St Anthony's. They were caught by the workers who brought them into the hall. We asked then where they came from. They told us they were at the Labour Department when two white guys came and asked if they wanted a job. They said yes, they wanted a job. When they were halfway they were given R4 each, told to distribute the papers and dumped. They distributed the statement that had been rejected by the workers.

We said to them: "Okay, you can go. But you must never take a funny job like this again. Sometimes the people could kill you. These people, as you see them here, are very angry. These people, as you see them here, are thirsty, they are hungry, they are starving, their children are starving, they are not working because of their bosses that fired them. Now you come with the rubbish statement which they rejected some weeks ago. The company has made fools of you. You must never do it again."

The following day the company telexed the union, saying they wanted a special meeting with the negotiating team. We went to the special meeting. They said: "We agree to these things. The workers must come back. It will be like nothing has happened. There will be no new contract and they won't lose anything. They must come back to their work."

We called it a victory. We planned to come back together the following day at St Anthony's where we would discuss how to go back to Dunlop. The next morning our official came and explained what the company was saying. The workers said: "Ja, now we are going back to our work again."

Now the big question was: how were we going to move? We were a large number – about 1500. There were some workers from Dunlop Sport at Mobeni who had joined us. We decided to walk from St Anthony's to Dunlop. We planned to go in fours.

We crossed Old Dutch, we passed the Indian Market in peace, then we crossed Berea. As we were crossing the police came with their vans. They grabbed the first four. I was in the second lot. They put us inside the van. Then all the workers jumped inside the van. They said: "No. We want these people in front only."

We said: "No. These are our leaders. We want to go with them wherever they go. Where are you taking them?"

They told us to sit down and forced the other workers to walk past Berea Road and the Technikon. They packed the people into an empty area known as Sparks. The workers started to sing and dance the toi-toi. The senior policeman came and asked what was happening. Bob Marie, the organiser, said: "Your people took the workers and stuck them there." The officer asked where the workers came from.

"These are the strikers of Dunlop," said Bobby, "they are going back to work at Dunlop."

"Okay, let the people go," said the officer, "back to their work."

From then on we didn't walk in order as we had done before. We spread all over the road, singing, coming down Williams Road. There are some women at Dalton Hostel who sell meat, homemade bread and beans with mealies (which we call izinkobe) and inside meat like liver. They were singing with us.

When we joined Sydney Road there were the staff of Dunlop: the clerks, computer people, typists were waving with their doeks, saying: "Come on, come on. Come on, come on." We heard that there was only one day left before they would have been kicked out, if we hadn't come back to work. We entered the gate and they told us to go to our departments. We went to our departments and arranged the starting time for the following day. We were paid our money from the week before we were fired.

Then they said to the negotiating committee: "Now you are back at work. That's fine, we are only going to do one thing. We are going to suspend the twelve who intimidated the people here at the gate."

We reported to the workers. The workers said: "Okay, if the company says that, shop stewards, go and tell them that now we can stay out for about a year. We've got our money; our pockets are full of money. We can solve our problems. Don't worry – we are going back to the forest again at St Anthony's, to use our machines there."

The company decided to drop that. They said they would not suspend the people. We said: "Okay, we will work." The following day we started our duty and there was happiness among the people.

The people who had been left behind, the staff like the foremen, couldn't look us in the face. We were happy and we didn't bother with them. We came with the new spirit and the workers were well disciplined. But some of the foremen were really hated because they had been so talkative when we were on strike.

Then there was an animal which the company called intimidation. Sometimes the electricity would just go out, especially at night. Then you would find somebody being beaten up. The union tried to stop that because it helped the company to get a grip on us. We had done a big thing; we had shown the world how we conquered Dunlop – so we shouldn't spoil our victory.

The company tried to sort these people out. One of the senior foremen was intimidated inside the company and pointed out the guy. The company threatened to dismiss him. After we had tried all our means to protect him we decided to strike.

We used the strike we called a 'siyalala la', which means we slept in the company's premises. We refused to leave because the factory belonged to us. We built it with our sweat and our blood. We lost all our energy to this company and so it belonged to us.

We slept all over the show inside the factory. We used to get up early in the morning, pray, relax again, go for a shower and dance the toi-toi. Then we went to where the container goes to load the tyres and to deliver the things coming from outside, such as raw materials and retreads.

When we came back we noticed that the company was pressurised by the aeroplane tyres because we found heaps of tyres needing to be retreaded lying all over. I don't know how the planes use their tyres but I have heard that if, for example, the tyres were fitted at Durban then it could only land at Johannesburg and then perhaps at Cape Town before new tyres have to be fitted.

We carried on with our siyalala la strike until the company decided to interdict us. On the day we were supposed to go to court we went back to work.

The work manager went to court. The magistrate said: "I know that we are here to talk about the strike. But I have heard that the workers are back at work. Which is what you wanted to interdict them to do. So I don't know what we will talk about."

The works manager came back very disappointed, asking the production manager why he let the culprits carry on with their work instead of going to court. The production manager said: "They have done what I wanted them to do. The only thing I want is production. I was worried – now I'm okay." Then there was a big fight between them.

One day the senior foreman came late, at 6:15am. He had to put on the lights in the department and start the machines because we were not allowed to do so. When we knocked off we noticed that they had deducted 15 minutes from our time.

When the workers started to grumble, I said: "No. Let's come back tomorrow to meet. That's where we'll demand our time back. If the senior foreman wants production we'll see him tomorrow." The workers agreed and we went home.

On Saturday morning we clocked in. When the foreman arrived we surrounded him and asked why he took 15 minutes from our time. He said he had been ordered to do so by the senior foreman. While we were talking the senior foreman came in. He was working at the mill department and the extruder department (our foreman went to Austria).

I couldn't control myself and said to him: "Ja, when you come to our department, you always come with nonsense." He said: "Hey Alfred, you mustn't talk like that to me." I said: "Yes, you always come with your nonsense. What have you done to our tickets, why have you cut our time?" He was very angry and I was cool.

I said: "I'm still asking that question. Why are you still coming with your nonsense in our department? You do good things in your department and then come and do funny things in our department. What is your problem?"

Then he started to grumble again and the workers started to shout at him. He said: "Okay, okay, okay."

He thought the trouble was over and went to his office. He didn't know that it was just the beginning because we despaired after that. All the drivers drove up the ramp to the office where we parked our forklifts. The rest of the workers were there already. We opened the doors and packed into the office like sardines. It was a very hot day.

I confronted him and said: "Now is the time. We have got two things and you have to choose one. If you want production today you have to give us our 15 minutes back. If you don't we'll go home and we won't give you a second today."

"No. I have done what I have done. I can't change anything. I have cut off 15 minutes because you were late."

"How can you tell us we were late when you were late. We came first. I know I clocked in at ten to six. How can I be late at ten to six?"

"You started work at quarter past."

"That was none of our business. You are the one who came late. You can't tell us that if you are late we are late. But if you want production then give us our time back. If not tell us now because we want to go."

"Okay, okay, okay," he said. "I'll go with you today but you must never do it again!"

"Yes, we will never do it again but you must never do

it again yourself – because you are the one who has done it first."

Then we left the office and started to work.

That was our experience at Dunlop. Always arguments, always problems. We struggled for everything we had. Nothing came from management to us as a special offer. They always wanted to exploit and in return we got nothing.

Around this time there were also strikes at Bakers Bread and at Clover. We did not stop at organising ourselves but spread our influence down the whole of Sydney Road, as the workers in other factories became organised. The working conditions in these factories were also bad.

Fourteen

1985 WAS A YEAR OF STOPPAGES. I remember the day we said we were going to pray. It was the time when people were killed at Hlobani by the vigilantes – who we realised were sent by a government body to do that dirty job. We marched out of the company at 11 o'clock. We met the workers from Clover, Breweries and Hart Ltd half-way, at King Edward. There was a prayer and we sang and toi-toied. Then we went to the company and went back to work.

There were also stoppages for the release of Mayekiso and his brothers. We negotiated with management but they said: "No. That is none of our business. The government always does these things because it is the government. If a person has done something wrong the government has a right to punish them."

We said: "You must talk to the government because you are part and parcel of the government. You create the laws together in parliament to oppress us. So go and tell the government that you support us when we want the release of Mayekiso and his brothers." The company said: "No way," so there was a stoppage.

In 1986 there was another strike, also around wages and working conditions. But this time they didn't want to dismiss us because the company had made a big loss by dismissing us in the first strike.

We demanded our pension fund and all our benefits back because we heard that the pension fund was controlled by the government to buy things to support the army. We opposed them using our money to buy weapons to kill us. They are fighting no war, but they are killing us in the townships, just as we go on our way, wherever they see us. We demanded our money back so we could put it where we wanted it. It was a real victory to get our money back. I put my money in the bank and fixed it there, for myself.

Instead of firing us they kicked us out of the factory, saying we were going to sabotage the machines. We told them: "We can't damage the machines because they belong to us. We are the ones who bought the machines with our sweat, our blood and our energy."

We didn't go to St Anthony's but changed the strategy to meeting three times a week. I was not a shop steward at that time; I had asked the workers not to elect me because I had other commitments to the organisation. I was busy up and down with my poems – reciting and encouraging other workers to write about their lives and experiences. We negotiated with them until they called us back again. It was a victory because we won some of our demands. We withdrew the demands that were not very important.

The management of Dunlop didn't want to learn that the people of today are not like the people of long ago. They used to recruit people for their culture. There was a senior foreman called Mzimba from Umkhomazi who used to recruit people who knew how to dance the Zulu dance. The company used to enter competitions against other companies like Hullets, Hart, Lever Brothers and Clover to get money. This way they exploited people double-time.

At Dunlop one day's work is like two days' work – you have to chase the electric rabbit. They want more production every day. If you managed to make 15 tyres a day, after a week they would want 20 tyres a day. If you managed to make 20 tyres then they would want even more. They'd never say this is enough. That is why they always had rejects – because workers were forced to work for the number of tyres not the quality of tyres. But when you made a lot of scraps they would call you to the office to be warned. They would always say it was because we didn't care, that we only worked to finish the day and get our wages.

In 1987 there were more stoppages. They always tried to swallow their words, to go back on their agreements. They tried to score goals but there were many goalkeepers who stopped the ball and sent it back to them.

This is the kind of company I can never forget.

Today, even though I've left Dunlop, I am proud of the Dunlop workers. They are an example to the militant workers in South Africa. I have heard that even when the company employed white scabs to replace the workers, some of the whites joined Numsa.

After forming Cosatu, a few workers didn't come to the Cosatu May Day rally but joined the Uwusa launch at Kings Park. One argued that he couldn't come to our rally because his chief was going to be at the Uwusa launch – if the chief didn't see him there he would be charged.

There they buried a coffin on which was written Cosatu,

Elijah Berayi, Jay Naidoo. They said today we are burying the Xhosa Elijah Berayi, the Indian Jay Naidoo, the South African Communist Party Cosatu and the ANC. After that we met at work and asked ourselves, how do we, as workers, see our organisation and how do we see this Uwusa, which wants to bury Cosatu? The question was: "Is Cosatu going to die or grow?" I am still asking that question today. Is it Cosatu or Uwusa that is dying? I still see that Cosatu is a giant while Uwusa is supported by pensioners. People were carried to the Uwusa launch by bus and train and came because they were being controlled by the chiefs.

I still praise Cosatu today and I will praise it until my bones are in the ground because it is an organisation and a half. It educates the workers from both sides, about the community and about the work place. But I haven't heard of even a single day that Uwusa had a sleep-in seminar to educate workers and have never seen them having a seminar for their shop stewards. The organisers, who are just Inkatha officials, just came to tell the companies to deduct money from Uwusa members and send it to Ulundi.

Rallies, yes, they have rallies. That is where they plan to attack Cosatu. The end is the beginning of the attack. They meet to plan attacks, not to talk about their problems at work. Their problem is Cosatu and the progressive organisations. I have never heard that Uwusa has won higher wages for workers. That is all I know about Uwusa. In fact, there is no thing such as Uwusa; there is only Inkatha.

Uwusa will never have a chance at Dunlop, even though the management supports Uwusa. There are still only those 12 guys that are on the executive of Uwusa.

Fifteen

I AM SURE THE DUNLOP COMPANY was very pleased when I resigned because the production manager always pointed at me. When I asked him what was wrong, he said: "There is nothing wrong but you are the trouble maker." I always asked him why he didn't come out with what was really wrong but he always pointed at me saying: "You are the trouble maker."

It started when we came back from the strike of 1986. We voted that if the company tried to make a worker sign a warning then everybody must go to that department and sign a warning. At the tube shop the manager gave a warning to three workers, saying that they were very slow. So we all went there.

When I entered the office they were talking and the manager was trying to explain himself to the workers. I walked in and burst into song. The workers started to toi-toi and some jumped on top of the table. What made me laugh was that when we were doing the toi-toi the production manager also tried to do the toi-toi. At the same time his long face was getting cross. I don't know what made him try to toi-toi.

After that he met me in my department and asked where I was working. I answered him: "At Dunlop."

"I know you are working at Dunlop but in which department?"

"In this department."

"Oh, you are a forklift driver."

"Yes, why are you asking?"

"I am just asking."

"Why are you asking me? Is there something behind this?"

"No, I am just asking."

After this he always pointed at me, saying: "You are a trouble maker." After that he was not my friend. But then I was not friends with anyone from management because we always had to fight with them. Even before the union came I used to fight with our shop manager because I tried to organise the drivers, as I did around the safety boots.

From then on it was cultural work for me most of the time. I had started composing izimbongo, which I was totally uncertain about – would the workers approve or not? They did. This influenced many more to emerge from our ranks. Nise Malange, Mi Hlatshwayo and I sat down and discussed our contribution thoroughly. From then on, without us even being able to understand it properly, a cultural movement launched itself all over Natal. I am glad that I had a role in stimulating its development. I am convinced of the brightness of its future.

The Wheel Is Turning – The Struggle Moves Forward

1.
Kill them all – the dogs.
Because, they say, they are becoming
    smarter.
They do not discriminate:
    the ignorant and the wise – exterminated
But still,
    truth remains unchanging
    it cannot change and lying
    causes anger
Our heads – held high
    they hide theirs
The struggle moves forward
    backwards never.

2.
The English arrived –
    and we were made ministers of religion
        teachers and clerks
    taught to be kind,
        humble, trusting and full of respect
    but ignorant of the ways our country was governed
        we began losing
        whatever we cherished for hope.

3.
But the wheel is turning
        darkness – ending
        daytime – beginning
        the light has come

Come freedom
> truth is unchanging
> its colours are stark

The end of your nights of lying
> is here

Surely you can see for yourselves ...

Return
> what is not yours
> the rightful owners are demanding it back.

4.
The struggle moves forward
> backwards never
> the wagon wheels turn
>> and their sound's echo
>> can be heard in our hearts and our souls:
> the rightful owner of the coat
>> stands freezing
>> rain soaking his bones
>> shredded by frost and cold winds

But you? You are smug
For your children? Only the best
and he? the crumbs
> and troubles
a stranger
> coatless in his rightful place.

5.
You were deceived
> by the first man
> who uttered:

"It is enough ... I'm satisfied"

since then you sat content and comfortable.
I use similar words
    "It is enough" and,
    "you have enjoyed yourself too long
Now it's my turn
    return my rightful share!"

6.
The struggle moves forward
    never backwards at all.
The earth has been gulping innocent blood
    – the first blood spilled in this struggle
    the very same earth we fought to retain
    since then we have noticed your conscience pricking
    your heart has found no peace
    days and nights you use for pacing.

7.
You pace up and down
    as ammunition you cargo on innocent people
Coward
    you are smudging the prospects of light
Your Casspirs, your teargas and guns
    your vans and your dogs
    do not dampen the fire
    they feed it.

8.
Cowards
You avoid attacking people
    with weapons like your own
You fear them

But still,
>   one day you shall harvest what you have sown
>   cursing the day you were born
This drought infested earth
>   will feast on your blood
What you did unto others
>   will be done unto you
>   and your armoury of weapons
>   shall follow you down
>   as the struggle moves forward
>   backwards, never.

9.
And you – Special Branch?
Who will help you?
>   those who have helped you
>   have turned into murderers
>   turning you into a curse
>   on the road to our freedom
And you even turn onto your own people
>   killing them with your own hands
>   they say.

10.
But the wagon-wheel turns
>   the struggle moves forward
>   backwards never.
Your police and your soldiers
>   are sniping at all those fighting for freedom
>   but the struggle continues
The police are detaining and killing
>   freedom fighters

torturing people in unimaginable way
yet it does not weaken our struggle
our struggle is fuelled once more.

11.
So many people detained
    and so many people killed
    that resistance should have been over by now
But the wagon-wheel turns
rolling forward
    and the struggle continues
    Your rulers' merciless detentions
    and jails
    malfunction
    and the struggle continues.

12.
Impimpi remind yourself
    what you are going to do
    when we start taking over
As victory strikes
    your friends will desert you.

13.
Now we are your lambs for slaughter
We are a torturing game for your friends
    you look on and laugh at us
    when we demand our rights
    when we condemn exploitation
    and shout about our unpaid labours
        you lead us onto paths full of traps
        but your days and those of your friends

    have been numbered
    and your friends will gladly give you away.

14.

And then, when our children
    complain of their gutter education?
    you deliver them for slaughter
    too
    but remember you do not weaken our struggle
        it
        strengthens.

15.

The day is near
    when your murderous weapons
    will stand witness
    for the higher judges of truth
    who won't be bribed with your money
    and then the filth of your deeds
    will become known
Then we shall clasp you with
    the steady grip of our hands.

16.

Soldiers
    murderers
    you have made orphans of us
    with your guns
You gain your rewards
    and respect
    for showing no mercy
    and lacking in conscience

You continue your routine
> of cruelty
But you can't see
> that it is our struggle
> you're making more respectable daily
> as we march forward.

17.
In the graveyards
and under black clouds
> people bury their loved ones
> – mourning and shedding their tears
>> yet it bothers you little
>> you do not sympathise
>> you show no remorse
>> you pretend to demonstrate bravery
>> your rifles are lifted as you snipe at some more
>> defenceless people
>> unable to fight back.

18.
They had them all killed –
like dogs
they are becoming smarter
they did not discriminate
between the wise or the fools
it matters little whether in celebration
in tears of in prayer
it is all the same,
all game for some sniping
after all they are getting smarter.

19.
When we gather,
    singing and orating our movement's slogans,
    we know
    that the souls of the people you have killed
    are with us in the struggle
Your tyranny cannot overpower our struggle
    ours continues going forward
        – backwards never
        the wheel is turning
        by tomorrow you shall be trying to flee
        but you shall be eating dust
        stamped to the ground like a snake
        – a trying punishment awaits you.

20.
The wheel is turning
Oppressor – wake up!
Beware and be conscious of what you are up to
Tomorrow the throne you occupy
    will become just another seat for others
    the others whom you hate
    will not allow you to forget their injuries
    which you have inflicted
The wheel is turning
    and there shall be no mercy for those killing
    innocent children.
The wheel is turning
    freedom is nearer
    our strength and our dignity
    – increasing

we shall conquer
as your time is coming up.

21.
The struggle moves forward
    backwards, never
    the wheel is turning
    you can hear the creaks of its motion yourself
Day after day
    your gun's bullets
    pierce the bodies of more freedom-fighters ...
Piercing the bodies of those who shout
    that you have been enjoying far too much
    for far too long
According to your logic
    everything should by now have been sorted,
    quiet and under
    control.

22.
Even for those who did not look like an oppressor
    who ignored your actions
    and respected you,
        you are becoming a monster
        they do not trust you any more
        they do not address you as a friend
        you are becoming an enemy.
Even those who ignored out struggles
    have opened their eyes in horror
    because you do not discriminate
    and your bullets do not discriminate
    everyone's up for the killing.

23.
The blood of the people
    finished-off by Amabutho
    has also started to talk
    and to bear witness.
They also are not ashamed to be killing
    people in mourning or prayer
        no feeling of shame when killing our youth
    and people's eyes are opening up to the horrors
    in this state of thieves
    but they only kill flesh
    the soul remains alive
    and the struggle refuses to die
    the struggle move forward.

24.
Don't kill
    don't intimidate
    don't be an obstacle to freedom
    if you want the end of our struggle
        then grant the people what they want
        but you can't face this truth
        that's why you kill and intimidate
        that is why you have created walls of darkness
        where you torture all our leaders
        and all those who speak out the truth.

25.
The wheel is turning
    the struggle moves forward
    backwards, never
the day is drawing closer

when not a single person shall again
be killed by your bullets
but the people you have killed –
> their blood sucked dry
> by this drought-stricken earth,
all those killed by amabutho
they will rise up from the graveyards
> and with their bare hands
> shall tear you to shreds
But you will not die
You will wish you were dead
> but you won't be.

26.
The wheel is turning
> the struggle moves forward
> backwards never
>> your sun is setting
>> your days draw near
>> your friends, your allies
>> and your propagandists
>> they will desert you
>> they shall climb on platforms in front of people
>> and denounce you.
The struggle continues
> and your Saracens
>> your machine-guns and sten-guns
>> your aeroplanes
>> your Casspirs and your kwela-kwelas
>> your teargas
> shall not break our strength

Your day is setting
Maye, unto you that day.

27.
In this war
        that is being fought around us
        we are not turning back
        we are wading through blood
        of our kinfolk
    when one of us falls
    when one get
        detained
another freedom-fighter
        of the exploited is born.

28.
The wheel is turning
    the struggle moves forward
    fires are raging
    as the enemies
        are worried and cannot sleep
        and cannot eat
        for their stomach rejects food
        because of all the plotting to set us back
        because of the plans to put the fire out
we continue with vigour
we say: turn wheel turn
turn on
and the flames keep on raging
and the smoke worries them a lot.

29.
The wheel is turning
   the struggle moves forward
      we are not to lose strength
      we die on the one side
      we rise on the other
      and continue
      on and on with our struggle
      until you become mad
      a lunatic oppressor
      wearing garlands of tree-leaves on your head
      and trying to end your life
   because the struggle continues
   the wheel is turning.
we move on.

It was during the 1986 Dunlop strike, when we occupied the factory, that I composed and recited the poem you have been reading: about this wheel turning and the struggle moving forward. It was also after my friend Toto Dwaba was assassinated and found dead at Umtunzini Sugar Plantation. His hands, one of his ears, one of his eyes and his tongue had been cut from his body. He was the Durban chairperson of the Release Mandela Campaign.

    The other workers were very pleased with the poem. After a while one of my co-workers came and asked me to whom was this poem directed. I answered that the poem was not directed at anyone. It was rather a response to our situation now in the country. He said that I was lying and the poem was talking about the KwaZulu authorities and government.

    I said: "No, it can't be because I am quite ignorant about KwaZulu politics. And anyway the poem could not be against them because they are also being governed by Pretoria, and they also suffer like all black people in South Africa."

He said then that I should write something about the KwaZulu authorities. I said I don't see myself ever doing that because I am ignorant of all these things. My aim was to praise the machine operators, the turners of wheels in the factories, the roadworkers, the diggers of gold and our organisations through which we were progressing. He left me without saying goodbye.

After a Saturday afternoon workshop on a play about M'kumbane, at about eight in the evening I returned to my uncle's place, at Amauti, Inanda. My family said that there had been visitors looking for me who claimed to come from an organisation fighting against the removal of people from their places. They were looking for that poet: me. My family were worried because one of them had a revolver under his jacket and, as my little nephew noticed, the car had a Johannesburg registration number and a KwaZulu Police (ZP) third-party.

I told my kin that those people were no friends of mine and they should not cooperate with them. From then there were many more visits, which made me decide to leave home. I have been uprooted since then.

But I shall keep on praising my brothers and sisters in the factories and shops, mines and farms – and I shall praise no chiefs. Even though the harassment of people is growing faster, the suppression of open political activity has caused confusion, and even though ethnic divisions are re-emerging and life is getting harder. I hope we are known and are remembered, not as a breed of nameless numbers but as people who dreamed of peace, prosperity, togetherness and freedom from exploitation.

Alfred Temba Qabula

Africa's Black Buffalo

The bull that left its byre when still in its calf stages,
    who followed the rocky paths, followed later by more calves
    meeting on the mountain ridges longing
        for their mother, bellowing and longing
        as they never reached the promised pastures
        they were searching for,
    to live and graze irrespective of their colour.

The black buffalo selected by the other bulls,
To leave the kraal to be apprenticed
It followed secret trails
And the others did not see it,
They heard rumours it was gone.

Outside the kraal, among others it bellows,
The other bulls give warnings, saying, "it is enough" and "homecoming is near"

Apprenticed in Algeria and told to come back home
Spotted on its arrival by the others
    who explained that it was dangerous to their grounds
    and their families could not sleep at all.

They gathered, declaring it an enemy, declaring war
They seized it and forced it in isolation on the island of Patima,
They returned to separate it from its calves, saying,
    it is not safe enough
    from the island of Patima it bellows and the dust goes up

and the others get unrested by the dust,
each bellow shows more power
they throw it into further isolation,
on top of a mountain of fish
From such distance there it remembers its calves,
It bellows and the dust moves up,
    the calves hear and on goes their sturdy stampede
    even some of the others associate with the black
    buffalo's calves
    together they stir up the dust on the paths to the top
    of the mountain of fish.

The oppressor leaps and shouts
    that unfortunately, they will never be tolerated while
    still alive
But their stomachs are grumbling and running from worry
    their tails were grass-wet from excretions,
    but still they attack decimating all
    even the milking calves are kicked, stabbed by horns
    and finished.

But the day is coming,
The tall grass will be scorched
    and a new season shall start with no lies.

Calves from black, brown and white buffaloes are
    stampeding
    harnesses are cracking, the yokes are left behind
    they do not sleep at nights, they have no pasture to
        graze in,
    they do not eat because they have no pasture to graze in,
    they do not drink water,

   because the rivers were diverted and dried
 they are being apprenticed
 they are swaying and beating up dust
   shaking off suffering.

Be prepared black buffalo
 the weight of suffering is teetering upon our shoulders.
   to end
   a cruel life beyond belief.